Y0-BCU-887

To Jack Canfield

and your team

With Gratitude and

tremendous appreciation

for your leadership, support,

encouragement, guidance

and faithful example.

I hope you find in this

book something of value!

Dean McFalls, Stockton

(209) 914-1920   books by dean egmail

This is my first author's copy.
Some very minor changes are still
pending.

Delivered on Christmas

DEAN MCFALLS
TEXT AND ILLUSTRATIONS

See you in Anaheim!

Copyright © 2017 by Dean McFalls.

ISBN:	Hardcover	978-1-5434-2205-4
	Softcover	978-1-5434-1278-9
	eBook	978-1-5434-1279-6

All rights reserved. No part of this book may be reproduced or transmitted in any form or by any means, electronic or mechanical, including photocopying, recording, or by any information storage and retrieval system, without permission in writing from the copyright owner.

Any people depicted in stock imagery provided by Thinkstock are models, and such images are being used for illustrative purposes only.
Certain stock imagery © Thinkstock.

Print information available on the last page.

Every effort has been made to give credit for photographs used and to obtain permission where possible.

Rev. date: 06/30/2017

To order additional copies of this book, contact:
Xlibris
1-888-795-4274
www.Xlibris.com
Orders@Xlibris.com
752773

A Note Regarding the Title and Cover of this Book

The anthology you're about to read began as *The Triumph of Innocence.* You'll see that title in every year's adventure. The themes of victory for the underdog and the power of simple faith play out, in a unique way, in each of these holiday sagas.

Inspired in 1976 by William Blake's artwork, his poetry, and his *Songs of Innocence and Experience* -- and by a classic American Christmas story -- I launched an annual tradition that would last fifteen years.

It only made sense, then, to use my original title for this anthology. However, searching online for other works called *The Triumph of Innocence* (to avoid copyright infringement), I discovered something far from innocent. To avoid any confusion of *this work* with *that work*, I had to find a new name.

Delivery and *deliverance* are also themes that permeate the stories in this book.

And *Christmas*, with all it means to us, is in every case central to the varied ways in which *innocence* prevails and the *delivery* and *deliverance* take place.

I encourage you to be on the lookout here for every heaven-sent blessing -- and meanwhile to be counting the blessings which have come into your life because of the *coming-into-our-history* of the One we call Christ.

If this anthology re-awakens in you this awareness -- with perhaps some awe, wonder, and gratitude -- it will have succeeded. Even better: I hope that you'll be drawn closer to the God who drew near to us in Bethlehem.

As the later episodes (1978 and beyond) make increasingly clear, the deliverance so urgently needed is not only for individuals – as in *my* salvation, or *our* redemption – but on an international, a universal, even a cosmic level. Christ came, not only for *you* and *me* and *each one of us*, but to deliver **all of Creation**. [1]

These stories all begin on Christmas Eve and end with the dawning of new hope.

That explains the providential choice of such a beautiful cover image by the team at XLibris who've helped bring you this anthology. Somehow, that winter scene integrates the diversity of these stories with an image of light in the darkness, of warmth in freezing cold, of a new day in the

---

[1] *See Isaiah 65:17-25, Ephesians 1:7-10, and Revelation, Chapter 21.*

midst of night, and the marvel of unfathomable mystery unfolding in utter simplicity.

May all that is wonderful be fulfilled in your life, too. May the Star that drew wise men long ago guide you, also, to the rebirth of your God-given innocence in the One who never knew sin, yet came to pay the price for ours.

One more detail: Today, March 25th, is the ***Feast of the Annunciation***. Today, we celebrate that grace-filled encounter between Gabriel, the Archangel, and Mary, the virgin of Nazareth. He declares God's intent; she responds with her ***"Fiat": "May it be done to me according to your word."*** [2]

And with this, the Son of God becomes incarnate in the Virgin's womb. [3]

It brings me great joy to have completed this book — begun over four decades ago -- *on this day.* One could say that, after 40 years in the desert, this baby has finally

---

[2]   *Luke 1:38, New American Bible, or NAB. Scriptures cited will be drawn from this translation, commonly used in the Catholic Church, or from the Revised Standard Version (RSV), my preferred translation since childhood in the United Church of Christ. Two will be taken from the New Revised Standard Version. One (p. 59) is from the New International Version.*

[3]   *Isaiah 7:14, the classic prediction of the birth of Emmanuel, God-With-Us.*

entered its promised land. After an interminable gestation, this child has at last been delivered!

Dean McFalls, 2017, Stockton, CA, USA

Dean McFalls' journey began in Seattle, where he and four siblings were raised in the Congregational Church UCC. During graduate studies in theology, Dean joined the Catholic Church. He has served over the years in elementary and high school education, in the missions, in international initiatives for justice and peace, as a writer, and for twenty years as a Roman Catholic priest. He now resides in Stockton, California, with his wife and their son. This is his first book; he hopes that many will follow.

Delivered on Christmas: an Anthology

"Today, if you hear His voice, do not harden your hearts..." [1]

Table of Contents

Illustrations by Dean McFalls, based on his original drawings for Triumph of Innocence episodes from 1976 to 1985, as well as a 1990 Christmas card and other drawings from across the years.

---

[1]   *Psalm 95:8 & Hebrews 3:8, 15, New Revised Standard Version*

The people who walked in darkness have seen a great light; upon those who lived in a land of gloom a light has shone. (Isaiah 9:1, NAB)

Author's Preface

From childhood, as Christmas drew near, I loved hearing once again that beloved American classic called *"The Night Before Christmas"* (or, as it was originally titled, *"A Visit from Saint Nicholas"*).

Its lyrical quality and palpable imagery captivated my imagination, and beckoned me back into the wonderful world of joy-filled anticipation and innocent fantasy.

Over forty years ago, I began writing variations of the original theme. These followed the pattern of meter,[1] of rhyme, and of imagery so skillfully rendered nearly 200 years ago. By 1990, I'd given birth to fifteen of these verses. They began as humorous, playful stories with a moral. Later (with the exception of 1985's second story,

---

[1]   *See page 183 for a more technical discussion of this meter and its potency.*

1

the silly one) each episode dealt with deeper concerns in my life's journey and the world's chronic dilemmas.

Poetry and verse had always been my inheritance. My father -- and his father as well -- were skilled at weaving meter and rhyme with humor and insight. My earliest years also featured the rise of my favorite children's author and illustrator, Theodor Geisel – alias *Dr. Seuss*. And so from an early age, I tried to do the same.

The term "verse" relates to the structure of what you'll find in this anthology, but the stories I relate would be superficial (and ultimately tedious) were it not for the element of poetry. If the interplay of meter and rhyme makes a message more accessible, the question still needs to be addressed: ***"What, then, is your message?"***

Author's Point of View
(Shared by Countless Believers)

What I'll declare here will become evident to you when you've read any of the stories of this book written in 1979 and beyond. But in case there's any doubt about my faith-orientation, I'll state my case from the beginning.

For those who prefer to keep issues of faith and morals out of their celebration of Christmas, I suggest you just read the first, second, and fourth of this series. These were written in 1985, 1976, and 1978. You can even skip the rest of this preface.

I can promise you some degree of entertainment, but I can't guarantee happiness.

For the rest of you, please note that I've served ten years in faith-based occupations, three years as a missionary, and twenty years as an ordained minister. I am also trying, together with my beloved wife, to raise our three-year-old faithfully.

Before writing, my preferred means of public communication was what we call a *"homily"*, or in non-Catholic language, a *"sermon"*. With that forewarning, please continue reading.

The reason for my new season of life.

NOW WE HAVE COLD DECEMBER
WHEN TWILIGHT COMES AT FOUR,
WHEN THE ONLY CALLER TAPPING
IS SLEET UPON THE DOOR.
WHEN CITY FORMS AND FIGURES,
IN OUTLINE BLACK AND BARE,
SOFTEN AT DUSK IN THE DRIFTING
SCENT OF WOODSMOKE IN THE AIR.

MIRACLE OF THE CHIMNEY-TOP
OUT OF THE BURNING TREE
THE GATHERED WARMTH OF SUMMER-
TIME RISES, RELEASED AND FREE.
RISES ABOVE THE CITY STREETS
AND TURNS THE THOUGHTS OF MEN
BACK FROM THE TOWN, BACK FROM THE
COLD, TO SUMMER WOODS AGAIN.

Constance Ling -1950

A poem by the author's great aunt — his paternal grandmother's sister, who spent most of her adult life in a Anthroposophic community in Spring Valley, New York. The author illustrated the poem as a Christmas gift to her and the extended family. The likely year was 1973, when author lived in Idaho surrounded by woods and, in winter, deep snow.

The Purpose for my Poetry –
that is, for using words with substance and beauty

1) Substance and Beauty are essential when we talk about Christmas.

This holiday would not continue to evoke such deep emotion and generate such hope and yearning if its content were reduced to sugarplums and reindeer, to ribbons and a jolly old elf named Santa. Much less does the modern world's reductive, commercialized caricature of the "holiday" offer lasting inspiration.

Popular culture and secular society have never, *and will never,* meet the deeper needs of the human spirit. The hopes and fears of all the years are met, not in Hollywood nor on Wall Street, but in lowly Bethlehem, in the crowded stable, in a manger filled with straw. They meet, today, in every contemporary echo of Bethlehem's simplicity. And, ultimately, they must meet in the human heart.

2) The human heart was created by God with a craving for God Himself.

As our children are spoon-fed (rather, force-fed) Americana's less-than-satisfying holiday diet of empty calories, their spirits cry out for so much more. They yearn for nourishment capable of giving true life and restoring our God-given dignity.

Most of us know the true story of Christmas. Many of us consider the birth of the Messiah to be a faith-based matter of life and death for the whole human race.

We will never be satisfied with even the most delightful counterfeits and masquerades of popular culture. We look beyond the annual onslaught of theatrics and distractions to the ultimate, redemptive power of the Incarnation.

As each one of us allows that power to manifest itself in our own personal life-journeys, our own Christmas story is written, engraved in our daily lives.

This explains, to a large degree, the motive behind these fifteen variations on the original theme of *"The Night Before Christmas"*. They range freely through the personal and political, the sublime and ridiculous, the spiritual and the mundane. But their steady movement is toward the Light which delivers us from darkness.

3) I believe that what began as "my" stories ultimately became God's.

Progressively, increasingly -- *with the exception of the three I've placed first* -- these were generated from the gut – that is, out from the center of my being. It was as if a new child were being born every December. Often without my willing it, and usually when I had little time or patience for the pains of delivery, these annual productions would simply start growing, and growing, and growing. They would demand my attention until each became its own unique obsession. Then, once finished (and usually illustrated), they would insist on being reproduced and mailed out to dozens of family members and friends. *Remember:* there was at this time no Internet, nor did we have cellular telephones and instant messaging.

Given that in the late 70's and 80's I was studying and working in a very wide variety of locations and conditions, it's a miracle in itself that anything got written, let alone distributed. But this testifies to the urgency I felt to give these stories life.

With the exception of 1985's second episode, *"An Unwelcome Guest"*, I've presented the annual verses in the order they were written.

Despite their historical setting and references, all the sagas have a timeless character. And since history has a way of repeating itself, several of the themes have become, once again, relevant.

A Request for an Open Mind and Heart

You may or may not sympathize with the point(s) of view expressed in these stories. Please keep in mind that, in all of them, I was struggling with difficult issues that hardly allowed for simple solutions. This explains the unexpected twists of fate that punctuate the plots, often leading to reversals in perspective.

The introductions and footnotes are not just filler. They offer essential background and context to narratives which you might otherwise find inaccessible. Footnotes clarify points and vocabulary, sharing as well the scriptural references inspiring my compositions. Everything is included to give you a wider window into the deeper significance of what these stories were meant to convey.

Illustrations will gradually disappear as the book progresses. Your imagination will supply far greater images than I can draw – images more relevant to you.

Thank you, dear reader, for having opened this book. I hope and pray that your immersion in these verses and their message will enrich your Christmas celebration, bringing blessings to your life, whoever and wherever you are.

And please, by the way – try to digest these stories slowly, a bit at a time. They are meant to be read aloud. The alliteration, rhyming, pacing and meter are all intended to make the message more flavorful and easier to assimilate.

How this Book is Organized

To set the stage, we've begun by reprinting the original **"Night Before Christmas"**. This way, you can see the source of inspiration and the pattern of verse which provided the template for my annual variations on the old familiar theme.

Next, you'll see three of my more light-hearted and satirical verses. I'm taking the risk of putting the most ridiculous one first. It's the only story that doesn't fit within the organic, progressive development of themes. But it is fun, and demonstrates how anyone with time on their hands can toy with the structure and images of the original classic, to create something uniquely their own.

The remaining stories will be presented in the order they were written. I'd prefer for you to read them from beginning to end, the first to the last. But if your curiosity or preoccupations lead you to pick and choose, be my guest!

With heartfelt gratitude to all who have read and appreciated these stories over the past four decades, and with eternal thanksgiving to the One who sent His Son into the world, and to that Child who is *the reason for the season,* I wish you all God's blessings.

Mary of Nazareth, pray for us! It was you who first opened your heart and your womb to the coming of our Redeemer. Now help us, your children, to open our hearts, as well, and to echo your ***"Yes"*** to the Father's will!

And on this, the 100th anniversary of your apparitions in Fatima[1], let our ***"Yes"*** be echoed throughout all Creation, so that the purpose of your visits and messages will be fulfilled, both now and in eternity. Amen. - *Dean H. McFalls*

---

[1]   *Beginning May 13th, 1917, the Virgin Mary began monthly visits to three shepherd children in Portugal. 70,000 people -- among them many skeptics, atheists, journalists, and secular leaders, were present on October 13th for the final apparition. The miracles they experienced that day are well-documented.*

But far more important were Our Lady's numerous messages, several of which have been borne out since that day as warnings and prophesies affecting the entire world. It is my hope and prayer that this book, and the next I'm writing, will be available this anniversary year. If you, reader, are unfamiliar or uncomfortable with Catholic devotion to Mary, please read the last four episodes in this book (from 1987 to 1990). I also encourage you to read, as if for the first time, the first chapter of Luke's Gospel. For those who wish to go deeper still, I recommend the recently published "Behold Your Mother -- A Biblical and Historical Defense of the Marian Doctrines", by former Marine and Fundamentalist Christian Tim Staples.

Thank you. And may God bless you in all your needs and deepest desires.

The Original Story: "The Night Before Christmas" *(December, 1834)* [2]

Introduction: People my age and older in the USA grew up with a delightful verse, first known as "A Visit from St. Nicholas". Most, if not all of us, can't remember when we first heard it, or how it got so deeply embedded in our collective soul.

This was the "white Christmas" story that kept every child's eyes half open, half the night. It was the prevailing cultural backdrop to our traditions of setting trees, hanging stockings, and leaving something out for Santa to drink. No one seemed to question the scenario this classic verse immortalized. And why should they? It was just a story; albeit bigger than life. It didn't pretend to anything else.

Authorship is debated. It might have been Henry Livingston Jr. But most likely 'twas Clement Clarke Moore, who's reputed to have presented this to his family on Christmas Eve, 1822. It would first be published the following year, in the Troy Sentinel newspaper of upstate New York.

I include this original, as I stated, so you can feel the energy and excitement of what inspired and shaped my fifteen variations over the years 1976 through 1990.

---

[2]   *This verse is now in the Public Domain, able to be reprinted without permission.*

There are some very slight changes from the original spellings, to make this verse more accessible to readers today, but none of the words have been changed.

As with all verse and poetry, this story is meant to be read slowly, aloud, with feeling. May this classic remind you of the holiday's magic. If you want to explore further, countless beautifully illustrated versions of the story -- and variants -- can be found online .

'Twas the night before Christmas, when all through the
  house, not a creature was stirring, not even a mouse.
The stockings were hung by the chimney with care,
  in hopes that Saint Nicholas soon would be there.

The children were nestled all snug in their beds,
  while visions of sugar-plums danced in their heads.
And mamma in her 'kerchief, and I in my cap,
  had just settled our brains for a long winter's nap.

When out on the lawn there arose such a clatter,
  I sprang from the bed to see what was the matter.
Away to the window I flew like a flash,
  tore open the shutters and threw up the sash.

The moon on the breast of the new-fallen snow
  gave the luster of mid-day to objects below.

When, what to my wondering eyes should appear,
  but a miniature sleigh, and eight tiny reindeer.

With a little old driver, so lively and quick,
  I knew in a moment it must be Saint Nick.
More rapid than eagles his coursers they came,
  and he whistled, and shouted, and called them by name!

"Now, Dasher! Now, Dancer! Now, Prancer and Vixen!
  On, Comet! On, Cupid! On, Donner and Blitzen!
To the top of the porch! To the top of the wall!
  Now dash away! Dash away! Dash away all!"

As dry leaves that before the wild hurricane fly,
  when they meet with an obstacle, mount to the sky,
so up to the house-top the coursers they flew,
  with the sleigh full of toys, and Saint Nicholas too.

And then, in a twinkling, I heard on the roof
  the prancing and pawing of each little hoof.
As I drew in my head, and was turning around,
  down the chimney Saint Nicholas came with a bound!

He was dressed all in fur, from his head to his foot,
  and his clothes were all tarnished with ashes and soot.
A bundle of toys he had flung on his back,
  and he looked like a peddler, just opening his pack.

His eyes-how they twinkled! His dimples how merry!
  His cheeks were like roses, his nose like a cherry!
His droll little mouth was drawn up like a bow,
  and the beard of his chin was as white as the snow.

The stump of a pipe he held tight in his teeth,
  and the smoke it encircled his head like a wreath.
He had a broad face and a little round belly,
  that shook when he laughed, like a bowlful of jelly!

He was chubby and plump, a right jolly old elf,
  and I laughed when I saw him, in spite of myself!
A wink of his eye and a twist of his head,
  soon gave me to know I had nothing to dread.

He spoke not a word, but went straight to his work,
  and filled all the stockings, then turned with a jerk.
And laying his finger aside of his nose,
  and giving a nod, up the chimney he rose!

He sprang to his sleigh, to his team gave a whistle,
  and away they all flew like the down of a thistle.
But I heard him exclaim, 'ere he drove out of sight,
  "Happy Christmas to all, and to all a good-night!"

The Triumph of Innocence Part 10:
"An Unwelcomed Visitor" (December 1985)

There's little or no excuse for having written this verse, the silliest of my fifteen Christmas sagas. But 1985 had been a tough year, both globally and for me as well. I spent most of it in Europe, both east and west, working with a variety of groups to promote international understanding through what we called "citizen diplomacy". That year, I also wrote the extremely long and intense Christmas version (1985, below), so for comic relief pumped out this one the day after.

This has absolutely no right to be featured in the anthology. I've included it, anyway, as a prelude to the rest that follow. They will be increasingly sincere and serious. Please have fun with this one before the poetry and real drama begins.

Perhaps the best rationale for including this version is to give children (and child-like adults) permission to experiment with verse, meter, and story. We often grow best when having fun. And fantasy is a great companion of creativity.

More urgently, in a world preparing for nuclear war, I wanted to offer some alternative to total annihilation. Today's world, three decades later, is even more unstable. For parents, I suggest that, after reading this, you ask your children how they'd have ended this story. *How about you, the parent, teacher, mentor or role model? If you're still very young, what kind of future do you want to imagine, and to help create? How would you translate that into a story or an illustration?*

'Twas the night before Christmas, and all through the villa,
  not a creature was stirring -- *except for Godzilla!*

The children were hid in the chimney with care,
  in hopes that Godzilla would not find them there.

While mom, in her kerchief, and I, in my cap
  had just settled down with a club in my lap,
When what to our wondering eyes should appear
  than a huge set of teeth, with a throat to the rear!

And the ugly beast belched, and it let out a breath
  that was hotter than hell and as smelly as death.
And the teeth crunched my club! And they almost
munched me,
  but my wife served the monster her chamomile tea.

She had run to the bathroom and emptied the shelves
  of those pills that addict us, in spite of ourselves,
and, mixing the meds like a magical bullet,
  she dumped the whole kettle down Godzilla's gullet.

Now the beast fell asleep, and we dashed for the phone
  where I dialed New York at the sound of the tone.
(As we learned from the film, if my memory's not wrong,
  when Godzilla shows up, you'd best get King Kong.)

So we called on the army to track down the ape
  who was currently keeping his muscles in shape,
perched on the Statue of Liberty's head,
  and whispering something that made her turn red.

Well, somehow they managed to coax King Kong down,
  and within a few hours, he was shipped to our town
where he entered our villa, drank all of our booze,
  then examined Godzilla in his chamomile snooze.

"We'll wait 'till he wakes, then I'll kill him outdoors,
  since there's no way to move a dead 'Zilla of course."

Thus said our ape – and we took his advice,
  since to get King Kong out would have also been nice.

Well, it doesn't take much to imagine the sight
  of such God-awful monsters engaged in a fight
to the death – but no doubt harder still
  to imagine what happened in lieu of a kill:

For being a warm-hearted, gentle gorilla,
  King Kong became friends with his enemy, 'Zilla!
It seems that he realized he wasn't the only
  oversized creature who always felt lonely.

So they left hand-in-claw for a deserted isle,
  where I pray that they'll stay for a very long while.

And though our poor villa—and the state, by osmosis—
  still smell of Great Ape and severe halitosis,
we live as before, in our quaint, simple way,
  and relate every Christmas what happened that day. *So...*

If some demon threatens to eat you entire,
  using God's name in vain, and breathing hell-fire,
just call on the Ape with the gigantic heart.
  he'll save Christmas Day. And that's a great start!

In fact, we could hear him, as they faded from sight,
  crying out, ***"Merry Christmas, and to all a good night!"***

The Santa Cycle: An Introduction

Five of the fifteen stories in this book include Santa Claus.
He plays a key role in each -- even as he's been central to
Christmas lore for centuries. With the exception of 1980
(and 1981, when I didn't compose a story), the "Santa
Cycle" represents the first episodes I wrote: 1976, 1977,
1978, 1979, and 1982. In all five, I explored different
images, perspectives and roles for the beloved elf.

As you discovered from the Godzilla saga, the Triumph
of Innocence series broke from the start with standard
warm-and-fuzzy, sugar-coated Christmas fare.

My purpose always involved cracking open the shell
of holiday superficialities, in order to discover some
mystery hidden within. It's as if one has to break through
the myth of Christmas in order to reveal the holiday's
unfathomably beautiful truths.

Even Santa Claus can play an important role here. Far
from the "jolly old elf" I critiqued in the Preface, Saint
Nicholas was a real flesh-and-blood human being who
lived 1,700 years ago in Asia Minor. A generous and
courageous bishop, he suffered persecution under the
Emperor Diocletian, but never wavered. History was on
his side: the next emperor was Constantine. By 313, when

Nicholas was roughly thirty-three years old, Christianity finally gained legal status. Before Nicholas died three decades later, Christianity would become the Roman Empire's official religion.

Saint Nicholas' charity shone like a light in the darkness. Within two centuries after his death, churches already bore his name. 800 years ago, December 6th was declared his feast day. And before long, he would emerge as one of the most beloved heroes of faith.

As devotion to saints within the Catholic and Orthodox churches became a matter of controversy for other Christians, "Father Christmas" and/or "Santa Claus" took Nicholas' place. But the historical reality still shines through.

This explains why, in 1982's episode, Santa reminisces on his *"one thousand, six hundred and forty-odd years"* in service to children. Whatever his trials and tribulations, Santa's love for the young and young-at-heart still drives him on.

If you don't like my portrayal of Santa in one episode, try the next. The saint represents, for me, the true spirit of Christmas breaking through into our secular culture. As misrepresented as he is misunderstood, the beloved bishop still manages, through the testimony of the ages, to manifest his charity.

That's a characteristic he shares with his Lord.

For this reason, I will not tell my three-year old that Santa doesn't exist.

Let him make up his own mind. Besides, he's already more fixated on Jesus.

In fact, if we could ever speak to Santa, I'm sure he'd recommend Jesus, too. For this reason, the nine more serious episodes of this series follow that advice. They begin with 1980's drama, then resume again with the years 1983 through 1990.

By way of transition, then, to 1977 and the Santa Cycle, I'll offer a rationale for the existence of this famous, but elusive, celebrity -- and then, an archival surprise:

A Debate Concerning the Existence (or lack thereof)
of Santa Claus (by Dean McFalls, c. 1973, for his
maternal Grandmother, Florence)

"Santa Claus is just a myth, recalled around the twenty-fifth."

"Yet people of your favorite town claim they've seen this
guy around.

"Take the case of two young kids
   who swore they saw tracks from his skids
   in New York City on Christmas Day.
Or of the farmer on his way
   to Buffalo: 'That day,' he said
   'I saw something above my head.
It uttered **Ho, Ho, Ho'**, he swore,
   though next: 'Perhaps it was the roar
   I heard, made by a jet in flight --
   but with red light, on Christmas night?'

"However weak the evidence,
   you can't deny the existence
   of Santa Claus once you've read this:
Downtown, my children met old Kris
   and filed their requests for toys.
Will you deny these girls and boys
   that they encountered Santa Claus?"

But I replied without a pause:
   "I was the man you speak about
   who proved Saint Nick without a doubt.
It was I who dressed myself
   to resemble that beloved elf."

"You've proved my point!" my friend replied,
  "for how could you be satisfied
   to pose as a non-entity?"
The thought of this so frightened me
  that I submitted, peacefully,
  admitting that there *had* to be
  a Santa Claus. In light of this,
how could we not enjoy Christmas?

How could we deny our youth
  the joy of this enduring truth:
That once the one called "Santa Claus"
  was, in fact, named Nicholas
– a faithful shepherd of the poor,
  a real-life saint: of this, we're sure!
Instead of wasting time debating,
  we ought to all be celebrating!
And this is surely the best reason
  why Santa's perfect for this Season.

A Dramatic Surprise from Long-Lost Archives

I had finished the entire project of this book, and was waiting to review what publishers call the "galleys", when I happened upon a small box buried under others for decades. Inside that box, I found an unmarked envelope. And what to my wondering eyes should appear, but (among other cards, poems, and articles) my first formal effort at a variation on ***"The Night Before Christmas".***

This was, in fact, my first book. With nine pages of text, and nine facing pages of colorful drawings, bound together with red thread and featuring even a cover and title page, this little project will mark fifty (50) full years this Christmas Eve, 2017.

Reading it for the first time in five decades, I recognized the illustrations and story-line -- yet had forgotten that the book even existed. Below is the text, with a few slight modifications to maintain the rhythm or correct spelling.

Please note that, in 1967, cameras still flashed with a contained explosion of light, the equipment Santa uses was a popular science fantasy, his boots all the rave, and STP was a too-well-known logo for the premier formulae in motor oil treatment.

The Night Before Christmas '67
by (twelve year-old) Dean McFalls

'Twas the night before Christmas, when all through the place,
  not a creature was sleeping -- of shut-eye, no trace.
The cameras were hid in the tall tree with care,
  in hopes that fat Santa would not see them there.

The children were noisily gabbing away
  about the events of the following day.
And Momma and I had just taken with care
  our snug peeking posts at the foot of the stair,

When out on the lawn there arose such a roaring,
  I looked out to see what fate could be storing.
What should I see above our long-dead grass,
  but an old man with snowy-white beard and moustache.

Wearing a red suit with present-filled pockets,
  and flying around with two retro-rockets,
And shouting with an authoritive air,
  "Now, Prancer! On, Dancer!, we'll soon be there!
To the top of the porch! To the top of the wall!
  Now, fly away, fly away, fly away all!"

As, to escape hunters, flies a fat grouse,
  Santa shot up to the top of the house.
Then with a saw with the sharpest of teeth,
  He cut a hole there the size of a wreath.

I heard a peculiar squeaking-like sound,
  and in came Saint Nicholas with a bound.

He looked really cool in his red leather suit,
  from the tip of his cap to a black go-go boot.
His skin had the texture of finely-ground sand,
  and there was a leather brief case in his hand.

On it were stickers from over the sea,
  like logos from Asia and Rome, Italy.
  But the largest of all was a huge **STP***!*

I came to my senses and jerked on the cord
  that was rigged up where the cameras were stored.

Somewhere along the line I made a goof --
  there was a flash and familiar *"poof"*,
but for some strange reason a camera caught fire --
  which spread from the camera to a cardboard lyre,
which spread to the tree that went up in a blaze
  -- I could have warmed my hands there for days!

But no, I heroically scooped up some water,
  and threw it on the tree, which grew hotter
and hotter, and hotter, and hotter until
  poor Santa Claus could no longer keep still.

He scattered some presents around on the floor,
  grabbed up his rockets and dashed out the door.
Seeing the fire was out of control
  I cleared out the house of each living soul.

But much to my grief I had no time to go
  back into the house to save any dough.
Speaking of money: my heart really sank --
  I hadn't invested in one single bank!

Now we live in poverty.

The moral is: LET SANTA BE!

Lest the reader be disturbed about the apocalyptic ending of my 1967 variation on the Christmas theme, be forewarned! My world in 1967 had been shaken forever by the assassination of John F. Kennedy, the rise of the Vietnam War, and the cultural convulsions taking place everywhere.

In 1965, the summer our family moved to a new, less tranquil neighborhood, a new song rocketed to #1 on the charts. "The Eve of Destruction", sung by Barry McGuire, still plays in my head. Somehow, it captured an entire generation's fears and anxieties. Meanwhile, there were forebodings of economic turmoil.

Dedicated to my father, this verse was an early tribute to his enduring themes: be frugal but financially wise, invest early on, don't bury your treasures. He warned often of "shirtsleeves to shirtsleeves in three generations". This meant that I might well squander the opportunities and accumulated legacy of past generations.

Like the Prodigal Son, I stood a high risk of ending up with empty hands and belly.

Look at me now! If you purchased this book, you've contributed to reversing the trend. God bless you (or your benefactor) for this. And now, please enjoy the remaining stories of this book. The next one was composed nine years after the episode of 1967.

The Triumph of Innocence, Part 1:
"The Beloved" (December 1976)

Following two and a half years of intensive studies at St. John's College, Santa Fe, I needed comic relief. This morality tale toys with elements of the original Night Before Christmas, revealing my love for the work of William Blake (the author/illustrator of "Songs of Innocence and Experience"). It also evokes images and sounds from Macbeth's Act IV, Scene 1. But my intention was to look for a more positive, family-friendly outcome.

I hope that you'll take your time, reading aloud and enjoying the play of word sounds and unexpected twists of fortune.

May we all discover, somehow, someday, the secret of True Love.

Regarding my state of life: I was single, and would remain so for forty more years. But within the worlds of my fantasies, I'd find myself in a variety of situations. These will present themselves naturally, as you enter the scenes of the 14 stories that follow.

'Twas the night before Christmas, and all through the house
  not a creature was stirring – except for my spouse.
She was bent o'er a kettle of bubbling brew,
  while I, in my innocence, snored the night through.

Well into darkness she worked o'er the potion,
  which rumbled and tumbled with quite a commotion.
It boiled while she toiled, and together they fought

'till, simmering, glimmering, it sunk in the pot.

And she mused, *"It is you, Santa Claus, whom I love!"*

while I, in my innocence, snored up above.

She set that love-draught near the chimney with care,

in hopes that Saint Nicholas soon would be there.

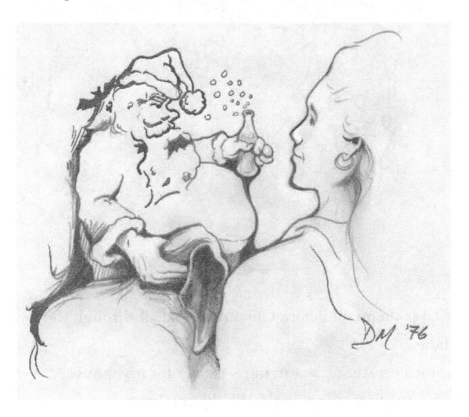

'Twas not that long after when Santa appeared,

with snowflakes and cinders and bats in his beard,

all pug-nosed and ruddy, with belly so vast

that he'd struggled some time in the chimney, stuck fast.

My wife, as she told me, recoiled in fear,
  but Santa saw only the drink that lay near.
He guzzled it down, and remained there in thought,
  while the potent love-potion went straight to the spot.

It rumbled and tumbled below in his bowels,
  and my wife thinks it strange that I slept through his howls.
But confessing, she said that its work was alarming –
  for quick as a wink, Santa Claus was Prince Charming!

With a gleam of affection, he turned to my wife,
  who had just about swooned with the thrill of her life,
And he said, *"Pardon me, but my heart is on fire!*
  I've got to go home to the one I desire!"
And putting his fingertip up to his nose,
  quick as a wink up the chimney he rose.

My wife almost died out of sheer misery;
  but then she repented, remembering me.

She ran to our room and threw open the door
  and scared me so much, I fell flat on the floor.
"What is the matter? Is Santa Claus here?"
  She replied, *"Please forgive me -- and swallow this, dear!"*

I drank, half asleep, and felt my gut groan,
  while my wife gazed, amazed, and released a loud moan.
Then she laughed, "You're a prince, but your beard is too thick!"
  and they've said, ever since, that I look like Saint Nick.

She's learned her lesson: to be satisfied,
  with any spouse who provides *love bonafide.*
And I am contented with features new found,
  for in Santa Land, loved, I *"Ho-Ho"* the year 'round!

The Triumph of Innocence, Part 2:
"The Warning" (December, 1977)

At twenty-two, I was obsessing on scripture, religion, philosophy, and the ongoing quest to find a spiritual home. Saint Augustine's *Confessions* and the writings of mystics like Saint John of the Cross had lent more impetus to my desire for purification and interior freedom. In this verse, I tried to dramatize the instability of a person still straddling the fence in their spiritual life.

Taos is a picturesque town not far from Santa Fe. Famed for its artistic community, it was also known as a place where people could still live as if the 1960's and 70's had never crossed the horizon. As for the "skins", this is a reference, not to any person, but to the instruments they played. If you read this verse loud enough, you'll hear those drums come to life once again.

You might also ask yourself: who and what played a key role in my conversion? Or if your conversion is still a work in progress (as is mine), what do you need to complete the work that's already begun? (See Philippians 1:6).

Self-portrait of the author from 1973

'Twas the night before Christmas, and all through the house
  boomed the drumming produced by some hippies from
  Taos.
I rolled and repented, remembering my sins,
  assuming doom boomed from the room with the skins.

For over an hour, I'd tried to ignore
  this pounding, resounding, which came through the door
- Nay, it rumbled the walls and it rattled my bed,
  while visions of wrongdoings crept through my head

– Nay, they beat at my brains and left me no peace,
  'till I prayed to Saint Nick that this drumming would cease.
For I knew that he'd witnessed my arrogant folly,
  and feared he'd appear in a mood far from jolly.

And lo, it was dark, and I, cold as ice,
  knew no cover, nor lover, for warmth could suffice.

Then, all at once, the drums boomed no more,
  and I heard only footsteps traversing the floor,
They stomped up the stairway, drew near to my room,
  while I pictured myself in a tomb's dismal gloom.

Next I heard thumping not far from my head,
and I bawled as I crawled to the foot of my bed.
"Y-yes?" whimpered I, *"W-what do you seek?"*
as I cringed at the curses the knocker might speak.

As when the loud thunderclap follows a bolt
of close lightning, these words gave the whole house a jolt:
"Come out of your room!!" roared the voice of a man
-- *"I've got to go bad, but I can't find your can!"* [1]

"What?" shouted I, as I leapt out of bed,
and ran to the door with my face turning red,
"You've gotta go potty? What do you think?
that this place is a hangout for party and drink?

"I see you've brought friends, with their tom-toms for drums,
overtaking my home like a slum full of bums!
Did you think that the note saying, *'Come on in, boss!'*
was hung there for you, and not Santa Claus?"

But I swallowed my words, when I gazed 'round the hall,
for my visitors didn't seem drunken at all,
and recalling that wise men prefer not to fight,
I offered them all that they might spend the night.

---

[1] *In days gone by, this referred to the bathroom facilities or the toilet. That less-than-inspiring image reminds us, in a crude way, of what Saint Paul says in Philippians 3:8-14. At least the visitor is willing to acknowledge his issues.*

*"**Brothers!**"* I chuckled, "y'know I was jokin' --
   there's nothing I love more than drinkin' and smokin'!
I've wine on the shelf, and cards on the table.
   we'll carouse and debauch for as long as we're able!"

"No thanks," said the crowd. "We've a duty to do,
   and you ought to be with us – this job is for you!
The one from below sent a message to us
   that he's looking for souls to fill up the next bus
which departs very soon. Would you like to be on it?
   you're on Satan's list, so you'd best dwell upon it.

"Our drumming's a message from -- *yes!* - Santa Claus,
   who suggests that you'd best learn respect for the laws;
--That you realize you're watched, that your records are kept,
   that in too many vices you're far too adept;

"However, with drumming, and a vigilant night,
   we trust that you'll last 'till the dawn's blessed light.
And that, with God's grace, you'll miss Satan's bus,
   so that you might celebrate Christmas with us!"

I fell on my knees, and called for the drummers;
   the door was left open to welcome newcomers;
We boomed through the night, and we boomed loud and
clear:
   *"**Merry Christmas to all, and a blessed New Year!**"*

The Triumph of Innocence, Part 3:
"The Solution" (December 1978)

Following my graduation from High School in Seattle (1973), I attended a new wilderness program in the panhandle of Northern Idaho. There, we lived a rugged life centered in personal discipline and in assuming responsibility for one's actions -- ultimately, for one's own destiny. The headmaster, a former marine who taught counter-guerrilla warfare during the Vietnam War, favored limited government and an enlightened free market with a strong moral base.

This verse, written the year I returned to the Academy as a teacher and assistant administrator, echoes some of our conversations. At times, the debate got very heated. Whatever side we took, we knew that what we assumed to be true could change, over time. As one matures, so (hopefully) do our opinions and attitudes. Truth stands forever, but in this world, very few dogmas are absolute.

'Twas the night before Christmas, and all through the school,
   shone a bright glowing light -- mysterious and cool,
It grew in its blueness, and moved through the room,
   as a star in its wanderings drew from the gloom.

We sat, frozen solid with silence and awe,
  captured — *enraptured* — by that which we saw.
For the cool hue of blueness transfigured our place,
  and foretold the approach of an alien race.

How long we sat staring, astonished, dumbfounded,
  no one recalls. But a sudden hum sounded
and the light-rays amazed with their blaze every eye,
  while the star from the dark beyond hovered nearby.

That humans are prone to illusion, I grant —
  one can't believe all that effusive folks chant!
But the sight of the eye, and the light of the mind,
  informed us that this thing was not of mankind.

Perhaps there are people with imaginations
  which fashion, in visions, fantastic creations;
But nowhere on earth, no, not even at Boeing,
  can a man manufacture this craft we saw glowing!

As if in response to our wild conjectures,
  and sudden acceptance of UFO lectures,
a slab of the saucer slid slowly aside,
  and out stepped a figure, all stubby and wide.

One of us shouted – I can't recall who –
  and back into darkness the creature withdrew.
But quick as a wink, it returned to the door,
  and clustered around it were twelve creatures more.

We whispered in wonder and fancied in fright
  every possible cause for this coming by night;
and, meanwhile, the visitors huddled, and mumbled
  with voices of munchkins –all squeaky and jumbled.

How many hours crawled by in this way!
  How long it appears we were held in the sway
of wonder and fear! Yet the creatures went on
  with their curious babbling which lasted 'till dawn.

Finally, one of them drew from the crowd,
  snapping at them in a voice harsh and loud.
He shuffled our way and climbed up the stairs,
  while we, in our misery, whispered our prayers.

"Humans!" he shouted, ***"Come out of your hiding!"***
  His voice sounded strained, but its tone was inviting.
"Please do come forth! Relinquish your fear!
  We're not so unearthly as we may appear!"

We cautiously came from the shadows to face
  this lone messenger of an yet-unknown race.
And we realized, relieved, as we slowly stepped forth,
  that this creature was *human – no more than a dwarf!*

With this realization, another one dawned,
  as we glanced from the dwarf to the huddle beyond;
We exclaimed, *"Santa Claus and his helpers are here!*
  but where are his sleigh and eight tiny reindeer?"

Said the dwarf, "Santa fired his reindeer in rage
  when the government boosted their minimum wage.
He designed this replacement: it's powered by fission,
  and it gets the job done with great speed and precision.

"One hang-up, however, it its operation,
  is the need for much patience and cooperation.
Many elves are required; they must work hard all night,
  and they think that their pay is a sliver too slight."

"Oh, Lord!" said we all, *"What a sad situation!*
  Santa Claus badgered by unionization!"
"Yes," sighed the dwarf, "You can see them in strife;
  Santa must give them a raise — or his life!"

We stood there in sorrow, observing the crowd,
  hearing words normally not heard out loud,
seeing defiance wax ugly and thick,
  and weeping to witness the plight of Saint Nick.

But suddenly light dawned again in the voice
  of one of our number, who realized the choice
opportunity here, in this battle of elves:
  she said, *"Let's go North, and help Santa ourselves!"*

"Of course!" we exclaimed. "We work best in snow,
  and our souls soar the highest where icicles grow;
Our muscles are strong and our minds never sleep;
  we won't unionize, so our labor's dirt cheap!

"Let's go to the Pole and leave far behind
  the troubles and trials and tears of mankind.
Let these elves take our place – we'll leave them as prey
  to this world in which Christmas lasts only a day!"

Santa was there; he caught every word,
  and he thought, *"That's the greatest news I've ever heard!"*
Aloud he cried, "Come, children, enter my hold,
  for your wisdom is silver, your spirit is gold!

"As for my elves -- *these spoiled mutineers* –
  they can taste the real world for a couple of years.
If they can't bear its weight, they'll come back on their knees,
  if they love it, it's theirs, for I won't waste my pleas."

We moved to the ship, with its cool hue of blue,
  and away from the huddle of elves it withdrew.
But through the dawn's mist saw we several small trolls,
  as they scurried, ecstatic, to take on our roles.

In winter, it's easy to forget the old saying
  that grass appears greener where others are staying;
and if unions seem to you an unworthy cause,
  you might think again when you're working for *Claus!*

So…parents, beware lest you fall prey, beguiled,
  to an elf who comes home in the guise of your child.
But should this befall you, don't banish the troll;
  just show him the world and he'll dream of the Pole.

As for your children, they're up in the snow,
  and their spirits are soaring where icicles grow.
Someday they may tire of life in the North –
  but 'till that occurs, be content with your dwarf!

Triumph of Innocence, Part 4:
"The Three Gifts" *(December 1979)*

It's impossible to convey the comprehensive darkness I felt as the 1970's gave way to the '80's. Many of us concerned about the nuclear arms race, concentrations of lethal power, and the specter of an Orwellian 1984 sensed the storm clouds on our collective horizon.

For me, as I hitched a ride home to Seattle from construction work in Santa Fe, things were darker, still. Two depressing events in the life of our extended family and the oppressive winters of the Pacific Northwest dampened my outlook on an uncertain future. I left behind my work with solar-passive homes in beautiful Santa Fe and would soon face the closing of Idaho's academy, where I'd planned to work a second consecutive year. We would have resumed in the spring.

Meanwhile, the Old Testament's Book of Job still hung heavy in my consciousness. Job was a great and wealthy man of the ancient near East who lost everything -- then stood up to God. My senior thesis was dedicated to his predicament. I took the project very, very seriously. So it's not surprising that 1979's Christmas version would struggle to find light in the darkness of loss and discouragement.

Hope springs eternal. Though I wrote most of this in an icebox VW bus with temperatures near zero outside, part was inspired by the scenic wonders of a five-day hike in Utah's Canyonlands National Park. For me, the beauty of nature was always a sure remedy for depression.

As you read what follows, I hope you, too, find renewed reasons to carry on in hope, always finding light on the horizon, and new life in the Lord of Mercy.

'Twas the night before Christmas, and all through the service
  I was constantly stirring – agitated and nervous.

The candle-lit faces, in peaceful procession,
  the joy mixed with awe in a single expression,
served only to deepen my sense of despair –
  their lives seemed so wonderful, mine so unfair!

"They," murmured I, "have good cause to rejoice;
  they've comfortable homes and careers of their choice.
On Christmas, they'll revel in feasting and presents,
  while I and my children are living like peasants!"

My judgment was sound, insofar as the toll
  of a chain of misfortunes beyond my control
thrust our family from riches to rags in a year,
  and cost me both wife and a long-sought career.

"Mind over matter," my conscience would chime;
  "You don't mind -- it won't matter!" *But I minded, this time!*
I had always worked hard to transcend tribulation,
  but had been unsuccessful in this situation.

After the service, I walked all alone
  to the ramshackle shack that we'd learned to call home,
and rejoiced that the children were sleeping in peace
  - though I wondered if sleep was their only release.
And I questioned how merry our Christmas would be
  with little but emptiness under the tree.

For hours, it seems, I remained in this state
  of endless insistence in dwelling on fate,
when, almost in spite of my skeptical bent,
  I uttered a prayer only kids would invent:

"If miracles happen, let one happen here!
  Let Santa exist, and make him appear!"
I laughed at myself, reclined on the floor,
  and half-asleep, humored, I worried no more.

Suddenly, pounding began overhead,
  so loud that I ran for the door, out of dread;
And noises joined in of such strength and duration,
  the hut seemed to shake to its very foundation!

Finally, the stovepipe vibrated with violence;
  a muffled cry sounded, and then there was silence.

"Who's in my stovepipe?" I yelled, quite surprised.
  "I'm Santa, and stuck, as you might have surmised!"

I stared at the stovepipe for over a minute,
  amazed that a human could ever get in it,
and doubting like mad that a man thick as Nicholas
  could fit in that fixture -- *the thought seemed ridiculous!*

"I know it seems strange," said the voice from within,
  "that I, Santa Claus, could have grown so darn thin,
but it hardly seems proper to stop and inquire
  when the one whom you question is catching on fire!
Besides, who but Santa would ruin his suit
  when your unbolted door makes an easier route?"

It took all our strength, and an hour, I guess,
  to get Santa out and to clean up the mess;

But nothing was harder than trying to relate
  to a skinny Saint Nick who had lost so much weight!

"Life has been rough at the pole," he explained;
  "our resources there have been totally drained.
All output, no income, and soaring inflation,
  have forced us to shut down the whole operation."

"**Woah!** Next to your lot, my woes aren't worth mention!
  Perhaps you're the one who should get the attention!"
I said that, but inside, I still felt deprived;
  while my prayer had been answered, no gifts had arrived.

"I know your thoughts," said the saint's gentle voice,
  "but assure you that you'll have good cause to rejoice.
For in spite of no business, scant food, and poor weather,
  I've learned to bestow better gifts altogether.
You'll see for yourself how three gifts which I'm giving
  will help you to find a new reason for living."

I wanted to ask him, *"Just what can you do?"*
  But quick as a wink, up the stovepipe he flew!
And somehow, in spite of my thoughts running wild,
  I fell asleep soundly, and slept like a child.

Morning arrived, with the sun on my head,
  and the joy of two children who rushed to my bed,
singing and dancing, their features all glowing,
  their laughter unceasing, their hearts overflowing.

"Good morning!" I cried, *"You're a sight to behold!*
  But tell me, what news brings such joy to my fold?"

It didn't take long for my kids to relate
  the dream which *each* had, leaving both in this state:
They'd been shown the extremes that some humans endure,
  from the glut born of greed, to the need of the poor.

They'd witnessed King Midas, overwhelmed by his gold,
  and the lot of poor Job, by his friends unconsoled.
To the ends of the earth, and throughout all of history,
  they had travelled in order to see the world's misery.

This, and yet more, left them deeply distressed,
  and the lessons they learned were so deeply impressed,
they rejoiced to be free of both hunger and glut,
  and could see *Paradise* in the midst of our hut.

I couldn't help weeping to see their elation --
  but inside, I harbored a deep reservation;

and in spite of my need to be happily involved,
  I felt that my issues were left unresolved.

What was my problem? And whence, my reserve?
  I guess I felt strongly for those who deserve
better treatment by fate than it seems is their lot.
  - And the dream I was told only strengthened this
  thought.

I was caught in the labyrinth of unanswered questions;
  the counsels of faith seemed like mindless suggestions;
and with every objection I sought to defend,
  I found myself lost in another dead end.

Forgetting what Christ's humble birth was about,
  I sank in self-pity, resentment, and doubt.
When all that I lacked was an honest confession,
  I traded my faith for a swamp of depression.

My children, neglected, tried hours, it seems,
  to wake their dad up from his negative dreams.
But as much as I wanted to brighten their day,
  I was empty inside, and had nothing to say.

Later that morning, a sound from the door
  began as a whisper, then rose to a roar.

"Merry Christmas!" was shouted, and hand bells were rung,
  and in sweet harmony, many carols were sung.

My children ran forward to open the door,
  and in flooded friends from church -- *twenty or more!*
They were bent under presents, and loaded with trays
  stacked with fine food and drink that would last us for days!

They must have been planning this gift all December,
  for it turned out to be one I'll always remember.
Now were the chains of complaining undone,
  and I soaked in their warmth, like a seedling, the sun.

We partied in earnest from noon until four,
  after which we attended a service once more.
There, during worship, my sight finally cleared,
  as the dream that my children had seen reappeared.

Now, I saw more than a strong exhortation
  to learn to rejoice in our new situation;
I realized, as well, that where fate is concerned,
  both the good and the bad seem so often unearned.

And at last I remembered that one out of four
  of the people who brought so much joy to our door

had serious hardships with which to contend --
  yet had given so much for the sake of a friend.

Just then, the miraculous happened inside,
  when that part of me hardened by hardship just died!
And the space that it left overflowed with thanksgiving,
  so that *praise* equaled *justice* as a purpose for living.

If the Lord of Creation could humble himself
  to be born of a family with no worldly wealth
and to live with rejection, and die on a cross,
  then why couldn't I take a much smaller loss?

For once, I could grasp how the Lord could embrace
  a world of detractors who spit in his face;
and cry out in faith, when his Father withdrew:
  "Forgive them, for they do not know what they do."

Illumined within for the first time in years
  I could see with new eyes, washed clean by my tears,
And instead of the presents I'd gladly received,
  It was in Jesus' presence that at last I believed.

I joined with my kids as we rose from the pew,
  singing **"Joy to the World,"** and meaning it, too!
Three gifts had been granted, which meant my deliverance.

...Had I only dreamt Santa? It makes little difference!

I love the LORD, for he heard my voice;
*   he heard my cry for mercy.*
The cords of death entangled me,
*   the anguish of the grave came over me;*
*   I was overcome by distress and sorrow.*
Then I called on the name of the LORD:
"LORD, save me!"
The LORD is gracious and righteous;
*   our God is full of compassion.*
The LORD protects the unwary;
*   when I was brought low, he saved me.*
Return to your rest, my soul,
*   for the LORD has been good to you.*
For you, LORD, have delivered me from death,
*   my eyes from tears, my feet from stumbling,*
that I may walk before the LORD in the land of the living.

(Psalm 116:1-9 New International Version)

The Triumph of Innocence, Part 5:
"The Sermon" (December 1980)

Immersed now in an environment of prayer, theology, discovery and pastoral energy, my outlook was far more positive. Besides, here we were in beautiful Berkeley, California! From my dormitory room in the Graduate Theological Union, I could see the San Francisco Bay, the Golden Gate Bridge and, below, the expansive UC campus. Life outdoors was a perpetual, fragrant spring.

Despite my activities with Amnesty International and the cause of peace and justice, in this year's episode my preoccupation turned inward to the spiritual journey and the call to ministry which I had finally embraced. The world situation seemed so bleak. With so little I could do, it seemed all the more essential to put first things first. What good would I do anyone, if my life wasn't glorifying God?

I tried here, as with 1979 and poems for the years to come, to be honest with God about how I was feeling. We have in the Psalms, the Book of Job, the Gospels, the Letters of Paul and the lives of so many saints, great examples of transparency before the Lord. Despite our human limitations, knowing that we are infinitely less and other than God, we still voice aloud our anxiety and our frustrations.

What father or mother would want anything else from a beloved child? How else could a child face his or her fears and immaturities, in order, eventually, to leave them behind? Yet knowing the love of God, how could we have turned away?

'Twas the night before Christmas, and all through Isaiah,
  through Amos, Ezekiel, Daniel, Hosea,
through the prophets of old did I search for the gleam
  of a message to serve as the Christmas Day theme.

Just out of college, not yet ordained,
  head stuffed with knowledge yet still scatter-brained,
and here I was, graced by committee accord,
  appointed to preach on the Day of our Lord.

But what could I say to a huge congregation
  to stimulate minds and provide inspiration?
My head in the clouds, I was too idealistic
  for down-to-earth crowds whose lives were realistic.
Besides, how could any church burden a youth
  with the task of discerning and teaching the truth?

The midnight bells rang as I started again
  to rip up a sermon I just couldn't mend,

and in spite of my efforts to say something clever,
   by two I was burning another endeavor.

The fifth in this series was shredded at four
   to the throb of a headache I couldn't ignore;
and, likewise, the sixth, when at five the bells rung:
   seven pages of text out the window were flung.

When six o'clock sounded from out of the mist
   I scattered the last with a blow of my fist,
and, cursing my fate through a clenched set of teeth,
   I shouted in four-letter French for relief.

The silent reply pierced my soul like a sword
   'till with tongue firmly bridled, I turned to the Lord.
"God, who am I," cried my voice with anxiety,
   "to presume that I've something to say to society?
Who am I, that you called me with patient persistence
   to a minister's life from a normal existence?"

"You're so thoughtful to ask!" said a voice from the ceiling;
   "your questions reflect all the qualms I've been feeling.
For twenty-five years you've resisted my call,
   but now is the Hour; it's too late to stall.
Be thankful for all the attention you've gotten
   and churn out a sermon — so what if it's rotten?"

At that I grew angry, my face turning red,
  and crying, *"You write it!"* I climbed into bed.

Outside the sky brightened and inside I slept,
  as ever-approaching the church service crept.
But I, in my sheets, knew at last no anxiety,
  and the visions of sleep came in endless variety.

I dreamt of a meadow in sunrays serene,
  of morning-gold mist over life-glowing green,
In the midst of a garden exceedingly lush
  from the bliss of which whispered the warbler and thrush.
And the quickening waters which passed, babbling, through
  moistened the soil as a gentle breeze blew.

In the midst of the meadow stood mighty, a tree
  from which life-giving fruit could be taken for free;
But as yet there was no one who tasted its yield,
  and its fruit fell, uneaten, to waste in the field.

Not far away lay a gnarled tree, withering --
  from the blows of a double-edged sword it was shivering.
With stroke of a flaming sword angels had felled it,
  while weeping, a huge crowd of humans beheld it.

The humans were gathered, like shadows at night,
  'round a black picket fence that surrounded the site.
They had worshipped the tree that lay cast to the ground,
  and they groaned in despair as they shuffled around.
Ceaselessly circled these shadows, bewailing
  the withering fruit tree whose powers were failing.

And eons, it seems, passed by in this way,
  and the darkness grew darker beyond the great fence;
  Inside the morning-gold light grew intense,
yet the fruit that was life-giving rot where it lay.

Then, from the denseness beyond came the droning
  of Civilization, replacing the moaning
of mourning with action and motion unending,
  with ceaseless distraction in purpose unbending.

From one corner, music, its melody drunken,
  whose dancers leapt high, lifting hearts cold and sunken;
Elsewhere, commotion of buying and selling
  an ocean of items with beauty compelling.

And here was a person who charted the stars,
And there, someone worshipping spirits in bars,
And there was a couple whose lord was their passion,
And a people who spent themselves keeping in fashion.
And here was a conflict, and there was a war,
  as the noise of humanity rose to a roar.

And then, soaring over this vale of insanity
  wailed the voice of a preacher: "All is vanity!"

I awoke in cold sweat, shivering and pale,
  and I wept at the thought of this vision of Hell,
But thanks be to God that, energy gone,
  I fell back asleep, and the vision went on.

For a figure drew forth from the side of the tree
  bathed in light, and surrounded with life-giving power.
  It walked to the fence from the midst of its bower
unlocking the gate with a morning-gold key.

Then, with a voice like the sound of the sea,
  the figure cried, "Come, and partake of the tree!
Lay down your burdens, awake to the day;
  only turn from distraction and follow My Way!"

Suddenly, silence descended like snow
 on the noise and the violence boiling below;
And it seemed that the darkness retreated, appalled,
 as innumerable eyes sought the One who had called.

The silence remained, in awesome suspension,
 in the power of human hearts held at attention,
but no one dared stir toward the One who had spoken
 and in moments, the tension of silence was broken.

Knowing, the figure remained at the gate,
 alone at the threshold, yet patient to wait,
while all turned their backs on the gate-keeper's gaze —
 though they yearned for the fruit, yet they favored their ways.
And wild, the din of humanity grew
 while the gate-keeper waited for one to pass through.

Finally, His eyes opened wide and he smiled
 at the sight of the first one to enter — a child!
The youngster partook and was flooded with light
 and she cried for her friends to come forth from the night.

One of them heard her, then beckoned the rest,
 'till so many came that the keeper was pressed;
And they rushed to the meadow to taste of the prize,
 while humanity's chaos continued to rise.

A life-giving Body encircled the tree,
* and they danced in their morning-gold mirth endlessly;*
When they hungered, the life-giving fruit was in reach,
* and in thirst they found plenty of water for each.*

Though they lived in the world and shared in its trials,
* yet they dwelt in the garden of morning-glow smiles;*
Though as humans their lives were attached to the earth,
* yet their spirits soared free with the joy of re-birth.*

This time I awoke with a sense of elation,
  the sun in my face and within, inspiration;
And had I not glanced at the watch on my wrist,
  I'd still be entranced in that morning-gold mist.

As it was, I had slept through the nine o'clock chimes
  and the service would start when the bell rang ten times.
So I bathed and got dressed and then bolted a mile
  and -- *by the grace of God* -- made it in style.

The service unfolded with carols and prayer,
  and the Spirit seemed present in everyone there;
while the tide of expectancy swelled to a peak
  right at the time I was scheduled to speak.

Needless to say, when I woke up to dash
   for the church, I'd forgotten my notes in the trash.
But what did that matter? A vision was sent
   that was better than anything I could invent.

When I climbed to the pulpit and told them my dream
   the story poured forth from my mouth like a stream.
And I, by excitement so fully transported, would have
   missed the whole thing, had it not been recorded.

Later, I asked in an indirect way
   for feedback concerning the sermon that day;
And it touched me to learn that most found it inspiring,
   while as for the others, who felt it was tiring --
They slept, every one, and dreamt of a scene
   of morning-gold mist over life-glowing green.

The Triumph of Innocence, Part 6:
"Peace on Earth" (December, 1982)

Following my entry into the Catholic Church during Easter of 1981, I prepared to leave the multi-denomination seminary setting. With three years to wait before being considered for the priesthood (and a religious order), and with increasing concern about the world-situation, I decided to invest myself fulltime in work for peace, justice, and what we called "citizen diplomacy".

This verse wrote itself as the Bethlehem Peace Pilgrimage approached Washington DC. During ten months of walking from the Trident Nuclear Submarine Base in Bangor, Washington State, we pilgrims had ample time to meditate of the state of the modern world. Things were not looking good. The future was at stake.

The Trident program had become symbolic of an arms race out of control. Nearly the length of two football fields end-to-end, the submarine was capable of delivering up to eight individually targeted nuclear warheads on each of twenty-four missiles (for a combined total of 192 warheads, each with far greater destructive force than the bombs that devastated Hiroshima and Nagasaki).

Limited only by the need to feed over 150 crew and officers on board, the 18 submarines eventually deployed have presented an ominous threat of total annihilation (called "deterrence") to enemies of America and her allies.

In 1980's terms, the cost of each equipped submarine was over two billion dollars — not counting operations and maintenance. Meanwhile, the Soviets had been developing their own version, called "Project 491", or "Akula" (meaning "Shark"), or, according to NATO, "Typhoon". This, too, was launched in the 1980's. With these kinds of weapons, we had achieved "MAD" -- Mutually Assured Destruction. Now nations with nuclear weapons could boast of their combined ability to annihilate all higher forms of life on earth, many times over.

Perhaps the most offensive detail in the United States' Trident program was the naming of one submarine the "Corpus Christi" -- that is, the "Body of Christ". Despite widespread protests, this name was vigorously defended by the Secretary of the Navy (the Trident being "an instrument of peace"), by the Mayor of the Texan town bearing that name, and by the Republican senator from Texas who wished to "honor" the city with the submarine. Money speaks, and for many fear is a greater motivator than faith. Clearly, this naming was a sacrilege.

Lead by Archbishop Hunthausen, 500 people joined us on Good Friday, 1982, to pray for peace and to launch our pilgrimage. Twelve of us would ultimately complete the entire 7,000 mile, two-year journey to Bethlehem.

But the halfway destination was our nation's capital. Our arrival coincided with the march of Vietnam veterans for the dedication of their memorial on the Mall, the deliberations in Washington, DC of America's Catholic Bishops (where they wrote a pastoral letter on war and peace), and Thanksgiving -- the celebration of our nation's legacy of faith, freedom and dependence on God.

If any terminology or references seem unclear, I'd prefer you search the terms yourself. This will help you feel some of the distress we felt, year after year. In recounting, below, the dilemma our world leaders faced, I speak in all seriousness. This dilemma echoes on, today, albeit with different details and today's rulers.

Ironically, as I write this, renewed East-West drama between Russia and the United States has been revving up, once again. History does, sadly, repeat itself.

'Twas the night before Christmas, and all through the North
  one could hear sounds of cheering as Santa set forth
from a comfortable cottage, the elves, and his wife,
  for the ends of the earth and the trial of his life.

The snow was light-falling and a gentle breeze blew
  as into the whiteness the cottage withdrew,

but in less than an hour the weather grew worse
and the ice bit so hard that it made Santa curse.

A blizzard began, and a bitter wind blew
as into the darkness the whiteness withdrew,
but Santa, resolved, kept his eyes straight ahead,
and, coaxing his reindeer, he crouched in the sled.

"Gets harder each year," Santa sighed to himself;
"This is no job, I fear, for an elderly elf!
If it weren't for the children, I'd gladly retire
to the arms of my wife and a warm, cozy fire!"

It was not out of laziness, weight, or old age
that Santa preferred to stay home at this stage,
but instead he remembered the dangers in store
from a world that was arming for nuclear war.

It was only four years since the trip had been marred
by the loss of his lead to the National Guard,
who had shipped dear old Rudolf to Los Alamos,
where a nuclear physicist studied his nose.

Two years ago, they'd careened through the heavens,
  being chased from the States by three F-111's, [1]
and last year, the sleigh had been split by the razor-
  sharp beam of somebody's new orbiting lazar.

It seemed fairly evident, given the past,
  that this effort at gift-giving might be their last.

The blizzard increased, and the bitter winds blew,
  as higher and higher the eight reindeer flew,
But they broke through the clouds to the moonlight above,
  where the crystal-blue sphere blessed their labor of love.

---

[1] *Pronounced "F-One-Elevens". The F-111 fighter jet was deployed from 1967 (when the Vietnam War was at its peak) until the late 1990's. It evolved through many variations. As for a space-based lazar, this was one of the projects contemplated by President Reagan as part of the "Star Wars" escalation. So far as we know, such a lazar has never been orbited. But research continues, and a future for space-based weapons seems more likely than ever.*

    During the Reagan administration, many other sophisticated weapons were developed (or completed) and deployed. Among these, the most expensive and/or destabilizing for the arms race were the B-1 (Lancer) and B-2 (Stealth) bombers, and the short-range Cruise and Pershing missiles. Ample evidence existed, also, for the development of bio-chemical weaponry. We would witness, firsthand, the fierce opposition in Western Europe as the short-range (and possibly some bio-chemical) weapons were stationed along the Iron Curtain. These systems made the entire zone vulnerable to a pre-emptive first strike on the part of the USSR. (Footnote continues on following page)

Meanwhile, below, children restlessly dozed
  with their eyes searching everywhere, never quite closed;
For Christmas joy gave them new reason for living,
  and their friend, Santa, hope, in this season of giving.

But just then, a Pentagon man was bent, stooping,
  his nose to a radar, his red eyelids drooping,
when what to his wondering eyes should appear
  but eight miniature blips and a blip to the rear!

He hopped like a frog to the phone marked *"Attack"*,
  and he shouted his news as a man shouted back.
A dozen projectiles were launched for the sleigh
  at such speeds that the reindeer could not get away.

So, cutting them loose, Santa dove from the sled
  and in seconds the missiles converged overhead.

For hours, it seems, Santa fell through the air,
  for as round as he was, he was blown everywhere,

(Cont'd) Of course, other nations had their arsenals, as well. The Soviets (and to a lesser degree the Chinese) presented a constant threat. No advance in military technology went unanswered. Meanwhile, the specter of atheistic communism still loomed on both horizons. Those born after 1970 will never fully grasp how frightening were the ominous clouds that hung over the heads of previous generations. The next episode will try to instill greater awareness.

and around him, a million presents descended
  toward Earth — but none toward the children intended.

Deprived of his mission, poor Santa despaired,
  his vision of gift-giving fully impaired,
yet, forgetting his own life, he started to pray
  for the sake of those kids who would miss Christmas Day.

Suddenly, something appeared far below
  which resembled a rooftop all covered with snow,
and, right in its middle, to Santa's surprise,
  an opening showed that was just the right size!

Swimming like mad through the snow-thickened air,
  Santa just managed to land himself there,
and grabbing some gifts that had fallen around,
  down the chimney Saint Nicholas went with a bound!

So ecstatic was he at this new chance for sharing
  he completely forgot that he'd just been despairing.
"Ho, Ho, Ho!" He exclaimed at the top of his lungs,
  and, full of the Spirit, he sang out in tongues.

Now looks are deceiving, especially at night,
  and what looked like the ultimate flue at first sight
was a missile-tube's throat in a submarine's deck,
  left exposed, I suppose, for a last-minute check.

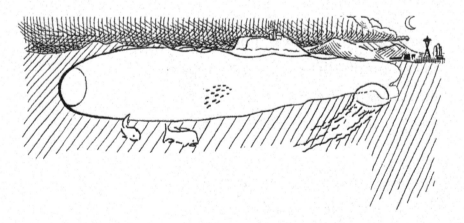

Somewhere below, in the submarine's belly,
  a missile technician named Nicholas Kelly
was dressed up as Santa — *he was made for the role --*
  entertaining the crew as they cruised for the Pole.

Now Nick had just split for the head without telling
   his mates of the urge that he found so compelling, [2]
so they sat there, debating his motives, perplexed,
   and began speculating on what would come next.

It was then that some men heard loud thumping and
grating
   from the tube where the missile for Moscow was waiting
for war. So they ran and unbolted its hatch
   and with flashlights, peered in to examine their catch.

Out flooded singing in very strange tongues
   and a man within laughed at the top of his lungs.

"It's Nicholas Kelly — just like I suspected!"
   Cried one of the crew when the others collected.
"I figured that such a respectable guy
   would turn out in the end to be Russian — a spy!
We'll teach him to sing — as he sinks in the ocean —
   and for sure we'll be given a Christmas promotion."

"Hold it a minute!" came someone's retort.
   "We can't prove he's red if he don't get to port!
Let's head for Seattle, go straight to the Brass;

---

[2]   *Here, "head" refers to the toilet facilities. The location of these in seafaring*
   vessels was often at the bow, or head, of the ship.

they'll reward us with leave and we'll party first class!
Who wants to spend Christmas Day under the Pole?
  This life on a Trident's no good for the soul."

Meanwhile, that fellow named Nicholas Kelly
  was hiding somewhere in the submarine's belly,
for he'd heard someone say that a spy had been found,
  and, being one too, he could not hang around.

Needless to say, in a very short while
  Saint Nick had been given a very short trial
and was sentenced posthaste when the quick verdict fell
  to a very long stay in a very small cell.

And the Pentagon ordered that, by Christmas Day,
  all the gifts that the missiles had blown from the sleigh
and had scattered from Maine to the San Andreas Fault
  should be gathered and stored in an underground vault.

This, then, my friends, might have been the conclusion:
  the sad end of Christmas in total confusion,
with nothing but emptiness under the tree,
  with stockings still hanging as flat as could be,
With Santa in prison, his gifts underground,
  and the Spirit of Christmas nowhere to be found!

But, thanks be to God, that, with morning's first hues,
   the millions of children who found out the news
resolved, one and all, in their naiveté,
   to bring Christmas back by the end of the day.

For as when a blast of wind spirits the fire,
   and myriads of sparks chase the flames ever-higher,
'till they climb as one pillar of light to the sky,
   so did millions of children unite in one cry.

And, as a spark in a hayfield seems tame
   'till in seconds it spreads to a great sheet of flame,
so, too, all around the earth, kids were ignited
   and under the banner of peace they united.

It seemed as if some unexplainable force
   drove these youngsters together, directing their course,
for into the streets of the world children poured,
   demanding that everyone lay down the sword.

They ran to the temples of every belief
   and prayed that from war they'd be granted relief;
and they streamed to the strongholds of power in each nation
   to demand that their leaders cease all preparation
for nuclear war. And they challenged the State
   to learn to let love be its guide, and not hate.

Finally, they cried, "While we still have a breath,
  let's begin to make choices for life, and not death.
Let all of our missiles be shot into space
  and the plans for more warheads, completely erased.
For the message of Christmas seems perfectly clear:
  if we lay down our weapons and pray, God will hear!"

Now, suggestions like these may sound too idealistic,
  and to experienced ears, unrealistic.
Yet somehow, the pleading of kids, in this season,
  served to melt with its warmth the most steely of reason.

For a moment or two, the world stood in silence,
  forgetting for once why there **had** to be violence,
and the Pentagon people just sat there, alarmed,
  for they could not recall why the hell they had armed!

Reagan, appalled at his efforts to squeeze
  every penny for war-making fell to his knees;
And even Andropov, when no one was near,
  felt remorse about Poland, and shed – yes! - *a tear.*

Well, as for what followed, it's needless to dwell
  on the world situation we all know so well.

But lest we leave Santa still locked in the pen,
  and Rudolf, still captive to Pentagon men,
the reindeer, still aimlessly flying around,
  and the presents still locked in a vault underground,

Let's remember with joy how our leaders repented
  – how Santa, his lead, and the deer were presented
recovered, released, and at last reunited,
  and the gifts all returned with a new sleigh provided.

And, finally, how President Reagan delighted
  to announce a great feast to which all were invited,
in honor of Santa and of youth everywhere
  who struggle for hope in a world of despair.

The White House doors opened, and children poured
through,
  and Santa, his lead, and the deer went in too.
There was great celebration, many carols were sung,
  and across this great nation, every church bell was rung.

Now the guest honored most had been laughing a while,
  when he said to his host with a fast-fading smile,
"Ronald, this banquet is fit for an elf!
  And I'm way-overeating in spite of myself;

The children are cheering for all they are worth,
  and at last it appears that there's peace here on earth!

"But tell me: what's happening after this feast?
  can we hope to stop monsters like Trident, at least?
Give these children a gift – put an old elf at ease --

by signing your name to the nuclear freeze!" [3]

Now, rarely before, since this nation began,
  has such a great burden been placed on a man
in the White House! And silence hung thick in the air,
  while the Spirit of God moved in everyone there.

Totally speechless, and ready to faint,
  Reagan felt himself lost in the eyes of the saint...
Then the burden was lifted! His shoulders went slack
  as if great loads of boulders were pulled from his back.
For it seemed that a legion of demons had fled!
  and his eyes streamed with tears as he gazed straight ahead.

But the silence that seemed to have lasted for years
  snapped! As the screams of a million fears
wailed like sirens inside of the president's head

---

[3]   *The Nuclear Freeze movement was gaining momentum as we launched our
     walk to Bethlehem. It called for a moratorium on the production, testing, and
     deployment of additional nuclear weapons. Opponents questioned whether
     Soviet compliance could ever be verified. Among them was Ronald Reagan,
     although his long-term stated mission was to greatly limit the nuclear threat.*

     *Ten years later, in 1992, President George H. W. Bush would declare
     a moratorium on nuclear testing. Secretary General Gorbachev had already
     declared a unilateral moratorium for the USSR in October of 1991. President
     Bill Clinton worked hard to foster further progress, even as the Soviet Union
     disintegrated into its constituent republics.*

-- and he seemed to be fighting them off when he said,

"Santa, I've never felt closer to you,
  -- nor to Christ! – nor these kids, than I presently do;
In a vision I've seen Heaven's gates open wide,
  With the singing of angels. – *But this screaming inside!!*"

The poor fellow whitened, and uttered a groan,
  and the next voice that stuttered was unlike his own:

"S-Santa," he smiled, "Let's b-be more optimistic!
  Your fears about war seem, to me, unrealistic.
For with first strike deterrents, we'll show beyond doubt
  that our country has nothing to w-worry about!

"We can talk later on of the f-freeze you've proposed,
  when the window of vulnerability's closed.
But until we've achieved an acceptable p-parity,
  let's not stake our future on c-communist charity!"

"May God save your soul!" shouted Santa out loud,
  and the room seemed to shake as he moved through the
  crowd.
"As for me, I'll be leaving – there's work to be done,
  and I've no guarantee that tomorrow will come!"

And he called to his reindeer, "Come! Night has arrived,
  and I can't stand to think of my children deprived
of their gifts any longer; Besides, I'm not sure
  just how long this official goodwill will endure."

That last part was whispered in words circumspect,
  but its message was nevertheless quite correct.
For whenever Saint Nick reminisced his career's
  one-thousand, six-hundred and forty-odd years
he could not help bemoaning what seemed such a crime:
  human beings had not grown a whole lot over time.

For as much as he loved them, he had to confess
  that for all of their charm, they could harm nonetheless.
They struggled so hard in the darkness of night,
  it was all he could do just to bring in some light.

This explains why such a warm-hearted troll
  as Saint Nick spends the bulk of his life at the Pole...
Yet in spite of his trials, he's able to cope,
  for in both young and young-at-heart, Santa finds hope.

It is hope that enables him, year after year,
  to continue his mission, in spite of his fear
of Destruction. For nothing enlivens him more
  than the child-like faith that, alone, can end war.

Someday the Nations will all pass away,
  and the Civilizations will rot, and decay;
The Towering Warlords will stumble, and rust,
  while their fortifications all crumble to dust.

But somewhere, beyond every old battlefield
  -- whether here or in Heaven will soon be revealed —
those still-young-at-heart, and the ones they inspire
  will forever be dancing, like sparks from the fire.

The snow was light-falling, and a gentle breeze blew
  as into the darkness the White House withdrew,
and, coaxing his reindeer, Santa crouched in his sled,
  while visions of gift-giving danced in his head.

And, weeping, he prayed like he'd never before
  that the Lord would deliver these people from war;
and, turning, he called to the last kids in sight:
  "Merry Christmas to all, and to all a good night!"

History -- with the fall of the Berlin Wall in 1989, and the subsequent dissolution of the Soviet empire -- has in many ways vindicated President Ronald Reagan. During his two terms in the 1980's, I had serious doubts. He was a charismatic and encouraging person, with deeply held convictions. But, as Eisenhower had warned in 1953, the arms race was spiraling out of control.

As later stories will describe, I witnessed firsthand the anxieties and resentment of Europeans. Caught in the middle between belligerent superpowers, held hostage by an escalating array of potentially devastating weapons, they were losing the autonomy they'd fought so long to gain. Many European youth didn't know where to turn.

I, too, found myself caught in-between. In November of 1984, worn out from two and a half years of non-stop journeys (mostly on foot), I took refuge for an hour in the American embassy.

I had come to Poland in another miserable chapter of their history. The weather, the countryside, and future prospects seemed bleak. With an afternoon free between visits to newfound friends, I stood before that embassy in Warsaw, looking at photographs of the Grand Canyon, of Mount Rushmore, of the Lincoln Memorial and, beaming with welcoming smiles, of Ronald and Nancy Reagan.

Inside, I indulged in a free bowl of Campbell's Tomato Soup with Saltine Crackers. That was all my system could handle at the time. But it was also one of the most memorable feasts of my life.

Following that hour's sojourn back in the country I'd left twenty long months before, I stood once again in the Polish rain. Soon, I'd visit Auschwitz. Then, within three weeks, I'd be back at work with the West German peace movement.

For a remarkable account of the relationship and collaboration between two key figures in the demise of Soviet Communism, see A Pope and a President: The Untold

Friendship of John Paul II and Ronald Reagan by *Paul Kengor*. Part of this saga includes the assassination attempts on both of these men, and their association with a mysterious woman named Mary.

The Pope and the President

Scott Stewart, Associated Press, 1987

The Triumph of Innocence, Part 7:
"On Holy Ground" (December 1983)

The arrival of our pilgrimage for peace in Bethlehem was, for each of us, absolutely unforgettable. Yet not all was calm and bright, neither in the world, nor in the land we call "Holy". This year's poem, the most multi-layered of all fifteen, links that morning of Christmas to the timeless history of struggle between light and darkness, between life and death, ultimately between the angels of God and the demons of the underworld. The outcome of this battle is certain in Christ, but it is not certain for humanity -- unless we, individually and collectively, choose to follow the One Who was born to show us the Way. He is the Prince of Peace.

A word to the wise: It's easy to get lost, time-wise, in this year's story. It moves quickly forward and backward in history. Hint: the first scene of this episode takes place in the year 2044 AD. But it's being told sometime after 2050. Don't expect science fiction here. The point is not to speculate on how things will look and work in another thirty-three years, but to highlight how all of history is affected by sin, division, violence and war. In this sense, the poem is a plea for a future in which our descendants can live without fear of annihilation.

If Jesus completed the work of Christmas (his Incarnation as Emmanuel, God-With-Us) and Easter (his redemptive Passion *and Resurrection) in thirty-three years, then perhaps in the same time, with his Spirit at work in us, we might complete that work he gave us, the Church, to do on earth (see John 14:12).*

'Twas the night before Christmas, 'round the old fireplace,
  where the flames brought new life to his withering face;
We were gathered 'round Grandpa in one wide-eyed stare,
  full of wonder and awe for the story he'd share.

For we'd heard that his life had been full of adventures!
  Yet it hurt him to talk, on account of his dentures.
For as long as we'd lived, he'd been quiet as a mouse,
  but tonight dear old Grandpa would light up the house.

Silent, he smiled at everyone present,
  while the fire, beside, turned his face luminescent,
and the only sound 'round us was crackling wood,
  'till at last Grandpa stretched up as high as he could,

And cried, *"My dear children!* You've gathered tonight
  for a nice Christmas tale – and indeed, you are right
to expect something pleasant from such an old friend!
  well, Good News you'll get…but not 'till the end.

"'Twas the night before Christmas, the year: '44,
  a time worse than any we'd witnessed before!
Nation rose against nation, there was war everywhere;
  people fled into panic and fell to despair...

"The whole world, it seemed, was being crushed by a curse!
  since the dawn of Creation, it'd never been worse.

"Oh, children! I don't want to plague you with fears
  -- God knows that I suffer to see you in tears –
But who, now, remembers how hard it was, then,
  to wake up each day to the same dread again?

"My Grandfather served as a soldier in France,
  and he barely survived when it happened, by chance
that before the explosion, he managed to dive --
  the grenade pierced his feet, but it left him alive.

"As he lay there that night, covered in blood,
  memories of Christmas past came like a flood,
and he dreamt that the soldiers had cancelled their fight
  to sing -- *yes! in harmony!* **'Silent Night'**.

"*His* grandpa had told him, the day he was dying,
  of a Christmas Eve, long before, when *he* was lying

in a foxhole, in Belgium, in the midst of a forest,
  and the soldiers had sung that song, too, in one chorus.

"They had called for a truce that would last Christmas Day;
  though it wasn't approved, they tried anyway,
and it seemed that the heavenly choirs sang along,
  making enemies friends for at least that one song. [1]

"Three decades later, not far from that scene,
  my Grandfather's heart rested, strangely serene,
as he bathed there, all night, in a heaven-sent vision
  of nations delivered from hate and division,

"The pain in his ankles and the loss of his friend
  were soothed by the hope that the war would soon end.
Though he never returned to those trenches, so bloody,
  he pledged, then, to honor the life of his buddy
who perished that day, by a full consecration
  of his life that remained to the God of Creation.

"When my grandmother passed, after fifty more years,
  my grandfather watered her grave with his tears,
then left his belongings to his children's estates,
  and spent his last decade beyond the bronze gates [2]

---

[1]   The "Christmas Truce" of 1914 happened across the Western Front during
      the first months of World War I. For this and other details related to the story,
      please refer to notes located at end of this story.

[2]   See page 104..

of a Cistercian monastery. There in silence
  he wept for a world chained in bondage to violence.

"And that spirit of peace-making passed to his son,
  and, through him, to me. And the life-giving One
Who had come to bring Peace to a war-weary Earth
  would lead me, on foot, to the place of His birth..."

"Grandpa, I'm lost! Could you please start again?"
said my cousin, confused, for she'd barely turned ten.
And at twelve, I confess that I had to agree:
So much information was too much for me!

But Grandpa just smiled, and a tear stained his cheek.
  "You can't know the pain that I suffer to speak!
It's not my teeth, kids, nor what seems like neutrality,
  but the trauma of memories steeped in brutality.

"How can you know that the peace you enjoy
  could have seemed so elusive when I was a boy?
Your country was arming the whole world for war
  and so were the Russians! But I had hope, for

"'Twas the night before Christmas when we laid down to
sleep
  in the field where, of old, shepherds tended their sheep,

where angels came, singing, and bringing Good News
  that the true Prince of Peace had been born of the Jews!

"Oh, we laid down to slumber like babies well fed
  -- after two years of walking, our bodies felt dead!
What a struggle to make it there, all in one piece!
  what a pleasure to treasure that sense of release!

"As I lay there, my memory flew through the past,
  reliving adventures – the first to the last –
reviewing the faces of saints left behind,
  reuniting with friends in the rooms of my mind.

"There was music outside from those who went on
  in a vigil for peace that continued 'till dawn.
They had joined in our pilgrimage, following the light
  of the bright Star of Bethlehem shining that night.

"I'd have easily joyfully sung the night through,
  but at long last I slept…and the next thing I knew:

"'Twas the night before Christmas, and all through the house,
  not a creature was stirring – not even a mouse.
Not a creature was breathing, not a body had breath,
  not a heart was left beating – *they were sleeping in death.*

"There was terrible stillness, save for the gale;
  there was terrible darkness, save for the pale,
pallid moon that shown through the smoke overhead,
  giving shape to the chaos – the ruins, the dead.

"Outside the house, it was drizzling pitch,
  and, around, all the ground was a huge, blackened ditch;
The earth was reduced to a smoldering ember
  - *Creation blown out in the cold of December.*

"This nightmare possessed me, like a morbid disease,
  and I felt death caress me, like ice on the breeze;
And the sight so distressed me, I awoke with a scream.
  - *Thanks be to God it was only a dream!*

"***'Thanks be to God!'*** I rejoiced as I wept,
  and my voice sang this chant 'till at long last I slept.
This time my dreams would retreat to the past
  to grope for some anchor where hope could cling fast. So…

"'Twas the night before Christmas, and all through the town
  there was no room left vacant – no place to lie down.
Two pilgrims were pleading, exhausted and chilled,
  while the innkeeper yelled that his rooms were all filled.

"They shuddered, confused, with a sense of despair,
   while the wind whipped as if it would drive them from
   there;
And they'd just turned their backs to the music inside
   when that solid inn door opened, suddenly, wide!

"'Friends!' cried the innkeeper, 'Don't go away!
   you can sleep with the animals – plenty of hay!'
'Oh, Lord!' uttered Joseph, 'I've lived through the worst.
   but to stick Mary there? - I'd build a house first!'
Yet Mary said, 'Joseph, he's trying his best.'
   she was starting to labor, and dying to rest.

"And she labored all night, in a Baptism wet,
   with her face bathed in tears and her body, in sweat,
and the stable was nearly pitch dark, cramped, and cold,
   and the damp hay was pungent with manure and mold.

"But Joseph was present to do what he could,
   and behind him, the animals, mute, understood –
For they gathered together as if they were praying
   and made a shrine of that stable where Mary was staying.

"Sometime near dawn, Mary's labor grew worse,
   'till in one long convulsion, the water sac burst,
and her Child was born in a life-bearing stream
   formed of water and blood. Thus ended my dream.

"'Twas the new day of Christmas; I 'woke to the sound
   of the vigilers singing and swinging around.
They were bathed in vermillion that came from the east
   praising, **'Glory to God in the Highest, and Peace
To His people on earth!'** – I felt my heart pound
   at the sudden awareness: *'This **is** Holy Ground!'*

"**Holy Ground!** – Where the blood, sweat and tears of the past
   of untold generations were fruitful at last!
Where the poor of the earth find their long-lost reward
   in the Year of God's Favor, the Day of the Lord!

"I could see how Creation was formed by Compassion
   – how our Lord was poured out in desire to fashion
a creature whose image could mirror His own
   – and how we, then, chose death, screaming *'Leave us alone!'*

"What more is the story of faith than the plea
   of a God we've locked out of our own history?

For whom water and blood are the only way in?
  Who must suffer and die to redeem us from sin?

"When darkness prevailed, God sent Light through the birth
  of Jesus, the cross-bearer, salt of the earth.
Christ gives us Hope – we who cling to the mud –
  and would wash us to Newness of Life with his blood.

"Well, we struggled, and learned to embrace the Lord's will
  in an hour when missiles were poised for the kill;
And when, taking peace-by-force, others destroyed it,
  we learned to make peace-through-peace -- and enjoyed it.

"The rest of the story is too long to tell,
  but I'll finish tomorrow, if y'all behave well.
Yet for now, I'll say this: there were many who cared;
  and, by the grace of God, Earth was spared.

"Well, back to my shepherds' field tent once again:
  I could feel something pleasant caressing my skin –
'Twas the warm light of Christmas that slowly grew stronger,
  'till I couldn't resist getting out any longer.

"So I threw off my blanket, drew open the door,
  and the golden sun spilled in, like coins, on the floor.

My eyes could perceive, in a wholly new way,
  Creation elated to greet the new day!

"Outside the grass glowed, as the dancers swung 'round,
  so I cast off my sandals and pranced Holy Ground!"

At this, Grandpa leaned out so far from the chair
  that he seemed to float up, like a ghost, in the air;
His bony frame shook from the weight of his feeling,
  yet his eyes rolled toward Heaven as he rose toward the
  ceiling.

And he cried, "My dear children, do you hear what I'm
  saying?
  I see you are nodding; indeed, some are praying!
Why, this lightens my burden — I can now go in peace --
  you can take on the world; I'll take my ease!"

Well, it won't hurt old Grandpa if he never finds out
  what those kids who were nodding were nodding about,
And the ones who seemed prayerful were already snoring
  - bless their young souls! They found Grandpa boring.

Why, we didn't even stir as the old man limped out…
  but one day we'd know what he worries about!

'Twas the beauty of Christmas that Grandpa would strive,
  in the face of rejection, to bring Christ alive!

His ancestors, through him, bore witness unending
  to the same Christmas message the angels were sending
when they sang to poor shepherds, in fields where *they* lay,
  and bid them to honor the Child in the hay.

Two thousand years later, the promise is clear:
  if *we* welcome Christ, we have nothing to fear!
There is no greater gift to be given on earth
  than the Life that is ours through the Christ-child's
  birth.

And as if to prove this, the Lord sent a sign:
  I glanced at the old man's hands as they passed mine,
and I'd swear they had punctures that smelled strangely
  sweet,
  and the fresh scars of piercing on each of his feet!

Oh, you Lords of the Earth! And you, New Generation!
  May you heed that old man – and defend God's Creation!
May we turn in repentance from bondage and fear
  to embrace Jesus' Way – for the Kingdom is here!

May the words of our ancestors echo in our mind,

and the message of angels reach all humankind,

For Christ has been born! Our Redeemer is here!

Merry Christmas to all, and a blessed New Year!

Footnotes, details, and explanations for "On Holy Ground"

1   *A formal ceasefire for the Christmas season had been proposed by Pope Benedict XV, but not officially accepted. However, realizing that they were in a miserable war for the long haul, soldiers took it upon themselves to bury their dead and exchange signs of goodwill. Reports agree that, in some cases, the Germans initiated this celebration with familiar carols, even singing some in English.*

Military leaders on both sides put an end to this goodwill in order to continue fighting for the defeat of their respective enemies.

This grandfather's trench was in Flanders, a region of Belgium, just north of France. The best description I've found online is at "www. longlongtrail.co.uk/battles/battles-of-the-western-front..."

Unfortunately, despite surviving the war, he seems to have passed away in his early sixties, just as the United States was entering the Second World War.

He must have been overcome with grief. But learning that his grandsons would be fighting, he wanted them to know that, in the bitter cold of winter's darkest days in 1914, light broke through on Christmas Eve along the Western Front.

Also, the second grandfather mentioned was fighting in France, at the horrendous (and last) major German offensive, the 1944-45 Battle of the Bulge. This spanned heavily forested regions in Belgium, France, and Luxembourg. On Christmas Eve, this battle was just nine days old. It would conclude a month later, causing perhaps a total of 200,000 casualties. No one seems to be certain of the exact toll, but agree that this was among the bloodiest European battles of World War II.

Total deaths caused by World War I had been around 35 million. World War II nearly doubled that – not to mention the long-term, indirect, and collateral costs of these wars on every level around the globe. This year's story, written from the Holy Land, briefly anticipates the nightmare of a total Apocalypse, but proposes another, more enlightened future. I pray that my son, and all our children, together with those yet to be born, will somehow be spared a World War III.

However, like many people, I have dreamt of the world's ending several times. This began with a series of lucid, full-colored dreams around the same time I began this series. Most recently, I dreamt of being in a rural village that was plunged into total chaos. It was night, and in panic people ran to the village's eastern edge to witness the sky turning bright purple. Suddenly, where the sun would be rising at dawn, a huge, semicircular section of sky turned turquoise blue.

Within the arc of this color stood, in full color and visible to all, the Holy Family.

They were standing in Bethlehem's stable, with the manger before them. But the Christ-child was also standing, now perhaps a few years old. Beside him, another child stood. I wondered to myself, "When Jesus comes again, he will come in glory. So what does this mean, that the Holy Family appears as in Bethlehem? And who is this child with them?"

Perhaps the message of the following episodes will help offer answers to the first question. As to the second, I'm still guessing. Maybe that second child beside Jesus stands for the innocent children whose lives were taken as Herod tried to eradicate the messianic King born in Bethlehem. Or perhaps that unknown child represents the role that our children have, even now -- and in every age of history -- in bringing the blessings of Christmas into the world in which they live.

2   The first grandfather's grandfather (who'd fought in WWII) had entered the monastery in 1995, according to this story. This marked, for me, the year of my ordination to the

priesthood. What for him was a consecration in prayerful silence was, for me, a dedication in service. However, I'd made retreats in monasteries regularly throughout the years that this book covers. We'll never fully know what difference the intercession of our monastic brothers and sisters makes in bringing light into the world, and in staving off potential disasters. We do know that the prayer of a holy person or community can move mountains and has great value to God (Matthew 17:20, James 5:16).

Though this poem was written in 1983, I've added reference to "fifty more years" to stretch the narrative historically. The first "grandfather" mentioned in this story would have been born around 1960, his grandfather around 1920, and the earliest grandfather around 1880. (Back in those days, people tended to marry and begin their families at a younger age than is now the case.) These men in the lineage were all first-born sons. Roughly twenty-three years old upon reaching Bethlehem, this first grandfather would now (2017) be in his late fifties.

Then why would he have aged so prematurely? We know his faith kept him young at heart. But in him and through him were living and dying countless generations of those who've been afflicted by war and by the human condition.

The truth to his aging, though, lies in the way this story has collapsed history. As I said in the introduction, the fireplace scene and the gathering around grandpa is taking place, not in 2017, but in 2044, one-hundred years after the Battle of the Bulge. The original narrator, "I" is (better, will be) twelve years old when this story is told. In other words, he and his sister won't be born until 2032 and '34, respectively.

For his part, the first grandfather mentioned will have reached 84 years old by the time he tells this fireplace story. My purpose here was to stretch the drama from the beginning of Creation until an uncertain future date which we may never reach, but hope will come to be. At the risk of omitting critical advances in human technology (will we still use fireplaces in 2044, or for that matter, dentures? In fact, will we still be here?) I wanted to anticipate a positive outcome for our planet.

This poem, then, becomes a plea for a collective future, free from catastrophes, for generations yet to be born. This plea has been expressed for 3,000 years in Psalm 22. Understood by Christians as a detailed prediction and description of Christ's brutal sufferings -- whose first lines he would quote even from the Cross -- this psalm ends with a prediction of deliverance:

I will tell of your name to my brothers and sisters; in
the midst of the congregation I will praise you:

You who fear the Lord, praise him!
All you offspring of Jacob, glorify him;
stand in awe of him, all you offspring of Israel!

For he did not despise or abhor
the affliction of the afflicted;
he did not hide his face from me,
but heard when I cried to him.

From you comes my praise in the great congregation;
my vows I will pay before those who fear him.

The poor shall eat and be satisfied;
those who seek him shall praise the Lord.

May your hearts live forever!
All the ends of the earth shall remember
and turn to the Lord;
and all the families of the nations
shall worship before him.

For dominion belongs to the Lord,
and he rules over the nations.

To him, indeed, shall all who sleep in the earth bow down;
before him shall bow all who go down to the dust,
and I shall live for him.

Posterity will serve him;
future generations will be told about the Lord,
and proclaim his deliverance to a people yet unborn,
saying that he has done it. *(Ps. 22:22-31, NRSV)*

One day we'll know more of grandpa's story -- and, if we survive, more about what happens between now and the future day when this story is being (will be) told. Until then, we remember that conflicts, violence and warfare take a much greater toll on humanity than anyone will ever imagine.

Christ was wounded nearly beyond recognition (Isaiah 53:1-5). Those who suffer with him, as Saint Paul says, fill up in their bodies what is lacking in Christ's sufferings for the Church (Colossians 1:24). That is, participating in the sacrifice Jesus made for us, they offer themselves for the building-up of God's people and for those in whom Jesus continues to be crucified (Matthew 25:40).

The Triumph of Innocence, Part 8:
"The Tower" (December 1984)

By August 1984, a second walk for peace (which I'd joined in Scotland) had reached Finland. There, blocked from entry as a group by Soviet authorities (who previously had promised cooperation), we divided into pairs and travelled within the Soviet Union to a variety of locations. Following adventures and misadventures in Leningrad, Moscow, and Odessa, I joined a Helsinki delegation to an international youth gathering in Warsaw, Poland. Then I travelled to witness, firsthand, the bleak state of depression created in that proud nation by an incompetent socialist government and the lie that was Soviet Communism.

Participants in a massive 1983 demonstration near Frankfurt against the staging of the Pershing II (short-range nuclear missiles) in West Germany. These weapons broke with previous treaties and made the nation more vulnerable to a preemptive first strike. Photo courtesy of Anna Stegmayer, Ludwigsburg.

A month later, I began collaborating with a West German woman's movement. In late October, I flew with their delegation to Washington, DC to organize presentations during the presidential election. We carried with us evidence and testimonies of the negative repercussions in Europe of the Cold War and nuclear arms race.

This year's poem was begun afterwards, and finished at Weston Priory, a Benedictine monastery in Vermont. It expressed my frustration about the fatal disconnect between faith and practice in so many places and people of the more prosperous world. Though it may smack of naïve activism and political correctness, at the time the perspective was essential. President Eisenhower had stated it eloquently in a speech following the death of Joseph Stalin thirty years before (that is, in 1953): the global arms race, even in a time of relative peace, robs humanity of what is most essential. A partial quote is included after this year's story.

For me, a generational obsession with East-West political and military relations would gradually metamorphosis into a greater concern for the impact these struggles have on the world's most vulnerable peoples, especially those living to the South. Some of my most heated debates were with leaders of American Christian churches. I was perceiving, more and more, the integral connection between the pursuit of military power and the subjugation of entire peoples to a market system which exploits and victimizes millions upon millions of innocent human beings. The perennial excuse was the menace of Communism and its ideology.

Throughout the 1970's and 80's, details abounded concerning the disproportional consumption -- and wasting -- of products from around the world by citizens of the "First World" – above all, the United States. Throughout what we called the "Third World" of underdeveloped, or developing nations, resources and the fruits of human labor were often unavailable to local populations. They were shipped off in exchange for goods, services, or finances that, in turn, would be funneled to those who held the positions of power and privilege.

Symbolic of this exploitation of the world's underprivileged were "cash crops" like coffee, bananas, chocolate, and tea (which I mention in this story), as well as the beef so coveted by Europeans and Americans. This was, by the way, before the era of mass production of cocaine. Opiates, narcotics, and marijuana were, at that time, much more in demand. Whatever the product, the mechanism was similar.

And the most effective means of maintaining this market system was the threat, or on occasion, the use of economic sanctions, interventions, or military force.

Understandably, I suffered from First-World guilt. I saw myself as a product and a participant in the subtle perversion of our deepest values by the thirst for comfort, security, and privilege. I hated the prostitution of what we held dearest for the sake of what we desired most dearly to have — to possess. And yet, we ourselves were being possessed in the process.

This co-opting of ultimate values to serve commercial interests was perfected by the advertising industry. It seemed, when I returned from Europe, that Americans were hypnotized by this trend and by the heavy filters of our media. Above all, "musak" (what we used to call elevator music, a kind of audio opiate or Soma), embodied for me this reductionist strategy, and thus I include it in this story.

Meanwhile, I fully understood the need to resist and, ultimately, to defeat the threat of communism, wherever it was being imposed on a populace that deserved systems of self-determination. In 1977, I'd even illustrated a book in Hungarian about the brutal suppression of that nation in the days of Stalin. The question was, however: "How to defeat communism, and at what cost?"

And so, as with all my Christmas verses, this one seeks solutions, but avoids a neat and tidy conclusion — much less a remedy that ignores the need for redemption in Christ. Thirty-three years later, I'm still dealing with the issues presented here.

'Twas the night before Christmas, and all through my sleep
  I had dreams that would make even mean people weep.
And ceaseless, increasing, they gathered, alas,
  'till my inner peace shattered, and scattered, like glass.

"Deliver me, Jesus!" I cried from my bed,
  and to shut out the visions, I buried my head.

My wife, now awake, sang a soft *"Silent Night"*,
  and she tried to convince me that things were alright;
But these ominous visits, which we scarce understood
  made me certain my life would be changing for good.

We had just settled down for a Christmas siesta,
  with our hearts warmed by song, and a lovely fiesta,
All the kids tucked in bed, with their teeth duly flossed,
  and the tree crammed with toys (at considerable cost),

And we'd prayed in one voice for our family and friends,
  for the system upon which our good life depends,
For conversion of Russia, and – of course! – for the poor,
  and World Peace – but I'd already started to snore –

And with snoring came sleep, and with sleep came the dreams
  that have pounded my heart for a lifetime, it seems.

Although I had yearned to be free, just one night,
  they streamed in, relentless, with no end in sight.

"Why, God," I prayed, "Is it so hard to rest?
  - I'm an innocent Christian, just doing his best.
I've got worries enough, what with children and bills,
  without being plagued by the world and its ills!"

But the Lord said, insistent, *"I'll make that decision!*
  You're awfully resistant for an 'innocent Christian'.
Your intentions are good, but your vision is blurred,
  and I'd like your attention to the following Word:"

With that we were sleeping – both me and my wife –
  while the Lord sent a dream that has since changed our life:

'Twas the night before Christmas, and, shrouded in black,
  Creation was waiting for day to come back.
She was praying for dawn -- for the light of the sun,
  for another return of the Life-Giving One.

She was waiting in agony, soon to give birth,
  while the screams of her labor vibrated the earth.
And dying, abandoned, she ceaselessly cried,
  that the Son might deliver the life trapped inside.

But as yet there was nothing but unending night
  to swallow her tears and to echo her plight.

And the universe, mourning, looked on with dismay
  at the sight of this tiny world passing away,
And they called upon Venus to break through the night
  as the bright morning star and a beacon of light.

But why was Creation so near to the tomb,
  and what was this child that stirred in her womb?
Where was the One who'd deliver new life?
  and when would the dawn put an end to her strife?

Well, *you* know the answer, my dreamer and friend,
  for the story's been told from beginning to end.
And the truths that have so long been shrouded in mystery
  will at dawn be revealed in the sealing of history.

But if thus far this dream has seemed vague and obscure,
  the following Word will be clearer, I'm sure:

'Twas the night before Christ's light, and all through this Hell
  there were many who suffered, but some who lived well;
And the few who lived comfortably strove to preserve it,
  while the others died on — though they didn't deserve it.

Now some of the comfortable lived off the toil
  of the poor at machinery, service and soil,
And they reasoned that "others could be prosperous:
  if they tried hard enough, why, they'd be just like us!

"Now of course God ordains that some suffer, however,
  for His Son said, 'The poor you have with you, forever…'!'"

And so forth they reasoned *(it seems they were lying),*
  while unfortunate people toiled on, and kept dying.

And ceaseless, increasing, the reasoning grew
  'till they thought God Almighty agreed with them, too.
And they knew one tongue, Money, and built a huge Tower
  using musak, and tax breaks, and nuclear power.

From this they shot rockets with weapons for space,
  and searched Third World pockets for a new marketplace,
Watching the enemy – and a small, struggling nation
  into which it might profit to launch an invasion.

And they worshipped the God who had blessed them so well
  unafraid that they'd made of Creation a Hell.

One day, a young woodworker challenged their violence:
  he planted an olive tree, then stood in silence.
"Nice fellow," they scoffed, *"But naïve and misled."*
  so they crossed an old hilltop, and left him there, dead.

Then the God that they hated came down in great wrath,
  and would wipe out the Tower that stood in His path,
But the Woodworker spoke – he who died and arose –
  "We created them free – let them see what they chose!"

And he called to the Tower: *"Your hour is here!"*
  - while the lovers of Power collapsed out of fear.
"At the moment of death, when your good life is done,
  you'll discover, surprised, that your time's just begun.

"You will carry forever the image of those
  whom your eyes would have seen, had your minds not
  been closed.
This Judgment is yours – for your judgment was free;
  You chose that your hearts should be frozen, not Me.

"I would gladly have raised you to Infinite Peace,
  like the billions who bore with your vile disease,
but the choice wasn't mine, and I'm sorry," he said.
  With that, the great Tower collapsed, crimson red.

I awoke with such terror, I fell to the floor
  - then yanked shut the curtains and bolted the door;
I dove in the closet and dropped to my knees,
  lifted hands to the ceiling and cried, **"Jesus, please!**

"Deliver me, Lord, from this terrible fate!
  I'm repenting, so spare me! - It can't be too late!"

Then breathed a whisper, a Word cool and still:
  "Don't call me 'Lord' if you won't do my will."

Somehow that message struck deep in my heart,
  'till I sank down in tears, and my world fell apart.
And there, in that closet, I died to my past,
  and the child inside was delivered, at last.
We danced in the One Light where spirits abide,
  and were joined by the myriads waiting outside.

Just then a pounding came hard on the door,
  and the sunlight spilled in where I lay on the floor.
"Oh, God! What's the matter?" My startled wife whined.
  "These visions have driven you out of your mind!"

"We can praise God for that," said I, stumbling out,
  and of course I explained what my tears were about.

For over an hour we danced — just like peasants!
  – Though the kids cried, impatient to open their presents.

Suffice it to say that our lives really changed,
  what with much more to live for, our goals rearranged.
Though we lost many comforts and the going got tough,
  we were wealthy with friendships, and rich with enough.
What incredible freedom! What a meaningful life!
  – and to start it on Christmas, I cooked for my wife.

But what could I do for my friends in the Tower?
  – well, I took them the Good Book. But in less than an hour
It was dropped in a slot marked: *"In case of Subversion"*,
  and then retranslated: ***"Today's Tower Version"***.

So I delivered a sermon I'd recently heard,
  saying, *"Listen, you worms, to the following Word:"*

"From South Africa's prisons to India and Ceylon, [1]
  from the ovens of Auschwitz to Beirut, Lebanon;

---

[1] *I grew up knowing the island-nation of Sri Lanka as Ceylon. This was the name used during the time of British occupation (1815-1948) and beyond. The conflicts mentioned in these four lines were in the news frequently during my youth. Were the poem to be rewritten today, I'd simply replace those references with others. But the underlying drama and trauma of humanity's divisions (made worse, according to Genesis chapter 11, by the greed for power symbolized by the Tower, and God's response) will play out until the end. Our task is not to build more towers. Rather, the prophets, and Jesus himself, call us to care for God's people.*

From Afghanistan's valleys to El Salvador,
  and from North Ireland to Iran and her war,

"Wherever the innocent hunger and thirst,
  and are torn by injustice: Christ will come first.
Everyone crushed by the burden of sin
  will be lifted to New Life when Christ comes again.

"But we who have always enjoyed being first
  will, in the Last Judgment, no doubt fare the worst;
For either we welcome the Son to renew us
  or the Night of Unending Regret will undo us.

"For the way to Corruption is easy and wide
  - either choose life or abuse life — you've got to decide!
To choose life, you'll lose the life your system secures,
  but the New Life you'll find is the kind that endures.

"So let's call this the year of God's Choice: '85!
  Let us Choose Life, and *Do* Life, while we're still alive!
In a time when humanity doubts her survival
  we can lead her to True Life. My friends, *that's* Revival!"

Well, my Tower-bound friends said, "We've heard this
before."
  and the biggest of them kicked me right out the door.
But in spite of their blindness and mindless perversion
  I pray every day for their final conversion.

And as for this couple? Suffice it to say
  that we're not quite Saint Francis and Dorothy Day! [2]
It's more than enough, still, to wean our way free
  from cheap chocolate, coffee, bananas and tea.

But whenever our worries grow bigger than life,
  I repeat with great comfort these words of my wife:

"We have all grown so greedy, we don't realize
  that the needs we are feeding are breeding like flies.
And since needing, indeed, is the human condition,
  we might as well take a decisive position
to determine which needs will make others *less* needy,
  letting go of those cravings which make us so greedy.

---

[2] *Dorothy Day (1897-1980) was a "radical" in the true sense of the word.
Following her conversion from a bohemian lifestyle, she dedicated her life to
service of the poor (co-founding the Catholic Worker movement), to works
of mercy, and to a courageous stand for justice. I see her spirituality as a
complement to the charism, or specific calling, of Mother Teresa of Calcutta.*

"So – if you please – take a tip from us mothers:
If you want to be free, make your needs those of others."

Well, I'm not sure exactly what all of that meant,
  so I'll leave it to folks with a mystical bent.
But of this I am certain: there's a New World in sight!
So…
Merry Christmas to all, and to all a Good Night!"

An Excerpt of President Eisenhower's Speech

Marking the occasion of Joseph Stalin's death, President Eisenhower gave his most famous address. In it, he described the fatal mistake of the path taken following World War II by the Soviet Union. But he also bemoaned the Western response, which was threatening to cripple the process of reconstruction.

(Cont'd) Dorothy's cause for canonization is underway. Both Popes Benedict XVI and Francis praised her commitment and work, holding her up as a model of authentic Christian charity lived out in an intensely political setting.

Eisenhower delivered this warning on April 16th, 1953. Having commanded the U.S. Army forces in Europe from 1942, and all allied forces in North Africa, then in Europe, he spoke from experience. It was he who had launched D-Day at Normandy.

When he delivered this speech to the American Society of Newspaper Editors, Eisenhower had just begun two terms as the President of the United States. With the death of Stalin, he envisioned a better world ahead. For this reason, the speech was carried live on radio and television, and published widely, at least in part.

The post-war world he describes – one of constant dread and paranoia -- was my generation's inheritance. Tragically, nothing substantially changed following Eisenhower's efforts, and by the 1980's, the arms race was out of control.

Referring to the Cold War between a paranoiac Soviet Union and the reactive United States, the president continued:

"…What can the world, or any nation in it, hope for if no turning is found on this dread road?

The worst to be feared and the best to be expected can be simply stated.

The worst is atomic war.

The best would be this: a life of perpetual fear and tension; a burden of arms draining the wealth and the labor of all peoples; a wasting of strength that defies the American system or the Soviet system or any system to achieve true abundance and happiness for the peoples of this earth.

Every gun that is made, every warship launched, every rocket fired signifies, in the final sense, a theft from those who hunger and are not fed, those who are cold and are not clothed. This world in arms is not spending money alone.

It is spending the sweat of its laborers, the genius of its scientists, the hopes of its children.

The cost of one modern heavy bomber is this: a modern brick school in more than 30 cities.

It is two electric power plants, each serving a town of 60,000 population.

It is two fine, fully equipped hospitals. It is some 50 miles of concrete highway.

We pay for a single fighter plane with a half million bushels of wheat.

We pay for a single destroyer with new homes that could have housed more than 8,000 people.

This, I repeat, is the best way of life to be found on the road the world has been taking.

This is not a way of life at all, in any true sense. Under the cloud of threatening war, it is humanity hanging from a cross of iron.

These plain and cruel truths define the peril and point the hope that come with this spring of 1953.

This is one of those times in the affairs of nations when the gravest choices must be made, if there is to be a turning toward a just and lasting peace.

It is a moment that calls upon the governments of the world to speak their intentions with simplicity and with honesty.

It calls upon them to answer the question that stirs the hearts of all sane men: is there no other way the world may live?..."

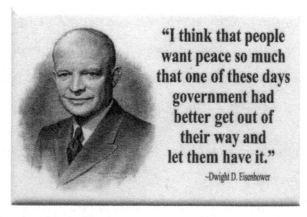

Credit: Peacemonger.org, Santa Cruz, CA

The Triumph of Innocence, Part 9:
"The Seventh-Story Suite" *(December 1985)*

1985 was to be — or so I thought — my last year of self-determined activities before I would — as I had supposed — enter the Society of Jesus. The Jesuits had been founded 450 years before by a converted Spanish soldier. I'd always been attracted by the order's discipline, their advanced studies, and their work in missions, social justice, quality education, professional careers and spiritual direction. But I had been witnessing things I did not appreciate. Not wanting to judge, I still had my doubts.

Meanwhile, a worsening world situation made me question the logic of undertaking ten to twelve years of formation to serve in a future that might well be reduced to cinders.

Joining two initiatives for outreach to citizens of several countries behind the Iron Curtain, I planned to expend my energies for political activity before entering the novitiate. But at the last minute, the vocations director demanded I drop those plans, or wait an additional year to be considered. By that time, I'd been invested for two months in what I thought was clearly God's will for me.

The vocations director told me I might not be the right material, anyway. Doubting his good will, I spent another six months in Europe, East and West, and in the Soviet Union. In France,

SEATTLE PEACE CHORUS

England, and Ireland, I gave presentations in churches and schools. But what I really wanted was to fulfill my vocation: I had been and done many things; I was called to be a priest.

My frustrations grew, and my blood began to boil, due to the institutions which, in my experience, perpetuated our world's problems, doing little nothing to resolve its deeper crises. As before, I saw myself as part of the systemic problem. I was still a beneficiary and willing participant in these institutions. And, as before, I saw no other way out but a total conversion, and a dedication of one's entire being to Christ.

This year's saga combines elements of the previous stories, now in epic proportions. If this were to be my last year on earth, I would go out with a bang. Please hang in there with this poem. It was written, again, on the road, and finished, once again, in a monastery. It tries to offer a real-world solution.

'Twas the night before Christmas, and all through our town
  not a creature stood still! – they were running around
like a loosed coop of chickens being chased late at night
  and I gazed from my roost with considerable fright.

The crunch of fast footsteps on fresh-fallen snow,
  the sound of loud pounding on doors down below,
and the shouting and honking that echoed around,
  left the Spirit of Christmas nowhere to be found.

But I, not one lightly to jeopardize life,
  climbed right back to bed and the arms of my wife.

We were seven stories up from the earth's broken sod,
  so much closer to Heaven, the dwelling of God.

We abode with our children in peaceful repose,
  unaffected – we hoped – by the world and its woes.

Always kind to our friends, giving alms to the poor,
  we led quiet lives of prayer, and asked nothing more.

Oh, of course, long ago, we had felt greater zeal
  for existence below, in the world they call "real",
but the specter of death and the trials of life
  had shred our ideals like a double-edged knife;
And so we'd retired to our high seventh story,
  where we waited in Christ to return in His Glory.

Taking refuge, therefore, in our lofty estate,
  we now prayed for the chaos below to abate.

Well, we'd hardly dozed off when a siren's shrill screams
  tore us back from the warmth of our Christmas Eve dreams,
and – lo! We heard friends in the streets far below:
  they were calling our names through the curtain of snow.

"Don't delay!" they cried up; *"You've got to come down!"*
  But the sirens resumed and their voices were drowned.

Grabbing our kids, we descended in haste,
  half-expecting disaster to somehow lay waste

to our town, and our home, and our family of five
  – so we prayed all the way to escape this alive.

Our friends were long gone, when we finally landed,
  and we shuddered to think that they'd left us here, stranded
to huddle, half-frozen, alone in the street,
  being crusted in snow from our heads to our feet.

And the darkness around us was deep as the sea,
  as thick as molasses, as black as can be!
Swallowed in infinite night, we shook there…
  – 'till a brilliant flash of white light filled the air!

As when lightning, immeasurably bright, splits the sky,
  or when fire explodes from a forest bone dry,
so shone, like a million suns, that celes-
  tial bolt, in its radiant glow, east to west.

Have you seen, on the screen, how a nuclear flash
  can reduce a huge city to rubble and ash?
Have you suffered through pictures of bodies burned black,
  or the sight of that child with a blood-crimsoned back?

Then you have an idea of the horror we knew
  on that terrible night, when the light pierced us through.

We were blinded, and flat on our backs in the snow
  - whether dead or alive, we were too stunned to know!
But with icy cold melt water soaking my shirt,
  I awoke to the fact that we'd only been hurt;
The still-frozen snow meant the town hadn't burned,
  and nothing suggested that Christ had returned...
Yet as I lay, stretched, though my eyesight was blind,
  a vision was vividly etched on my mind.

I had seen a great crowd from all nations, bowed down
  to a hideous beast with a five-sided crown.

All around it lay bones it had spat in the field,
  and over it arched an invulnerable shield.
Its left hand clutched money; its right held a sword,
  and it thundered, **"I AM!!"** while the crowd answered,
"LORD!!"

Then came this vision: a billion faces
  made up of all ages, all faiths and all races;
They were thin with starvation, and pale with disease;
  said a whispering voice from behind: *"I am these."*

And then the voice cried, 'ere this vision was done:
  "Why do you hide from my people, my son?"

Needless to say, I was deeply distressed,
  and those echoing words left me weak and depressed,
so that, speechless, I lay cold as ice in the snow,
  'till my wife, who was also blind, cried, "Dear, let's go!"

We groped through the darkness and rose to our feet,
  only hoping by chance to find friends in the street;
and friends we did find! - Our three children, in fact —
  somehow the great flash had left their sight intact.

They led us along at a shuffling pace
  toward a hill where the light had now taken its place.

When we finally arrived, there were sounds of a crowd
  (that is, whispering, sighing, and praying aloud),
And the voice of a woman who called us by name,
  saying, *"I am called Anna. Thank God that you came.*

"Tonight I was given a frightening vision
  and a warning that this is the time of Decision.
I told all your neighbors that Christ would appear,
  but you were too high and to hidden to hear."

She had brought with her clay from a far-away land
  which she mixed with her spit in the palm of her hand,
and although we resisted the balm she had made,
  she gently insisted, "Do not be afraid."

At last, with disgust, we surrendered each eye
  to the warm mud and dust that our nurse would apply,
yet as soon as that earth had been pressed, then washed free
  with a stream of pure water, our blind eyes could see!

At first, we beheld a great arc overhead
  made of six bands of colors, from violet to red;
The bow formed a circle, its ends coming 'round
  to be anchored as one in the dark, broken ground.

And its hues were intense, like the full moon at night,
  and its colors were pure, as from diamonds in light,
and its glow was so strong that it flooded our hill
  to drown the great throng that stood awestruck and still.

But more beautiful, still, was a figure within,
  of a young peasant woman with dark, olive skin.
She was wearing a crown, not of gold, but of light,
  and a long, flowing gown made of lace, pearl-white.

Her shoulders were robed in the dawn's early hues;
  in the folds shone bright stars against dark, midnight blues.
Her heels crushed a serpent that bled in the snow,
  and, from each, arched upward one end of the bow.

She cradled the tiny Christ Child at her breast,
  and He, in turn, cradled the earth to His chest.

Then said her voice, 'ere the vision went dim:
"This is my beloved Son: follow Him."

We stood in a spell, with our eyes full of tears,
  and though the snow fell and the ice nipped our ears,
to cling to that vision was our only desire.
  - Though our bodies were frozen, our hearts were on fire!

Day came in slowly, transfiguring clouds,
  and carols arose as its light warmed the crowds.
But I remained cold, and my vision went slack,
  so, letting the others move on, I turned back.

"Thanks, Lord," I cried, "for a beautiful show.
  but what did we learn that we didn't yet know?
Are your people now wiser? Has your light reached their
brain?
  Is the world any brighter? Is there any less pain?"

"It is good," said a voice, *"that you come, so demanding,*
  for my people seek visions, but not understanding."
I spun around, wondering who was the speaker,
  but my mind was in darkness, my eyes, even weaker.
The voice carried on: "Let this be your mission:
  to share what I tell you with all who will listen.

"In the days of the Great Flood, when Evil was purged
  from the face of Creation, my son Noah urged
me to wipe away even the option for sin,
  so a new and more promising world might begin.

"How deeply I yearned to free Earth from this bind!
  - To take back the choice which I gave humankind!
But to do that would only have made matters worse,
  by throwing the process of Life in reverse.

"Evolution and growth is the work of Creation,
  and Life to the full is its sole Destination.
To enslave human freedom would cripple the soul.
  - For when you return to me, I want you whole.

"I've made you unable to live to the full
  if you won't cleave to me with your body and soul;
The Paradox, then, is that I've made you free,
  but your true freedom lies in allegiance to me.

"I gave you my Pledge in the Covenant arc
  that life would continue, no matter how dark
and how petty your motives and actions might be
  - so if Holocaust threatens, *do not blame me!*

"What I promise is Life on a far greater scale,

and Love that makes lovemaking look strangely pale.
I give you a Nation beyond time and space,
   and Participation in Glory, by grace.

"I'm the Fount of Creation, in eternal birth,
   and I am Life, springing forth fresh from the earth;
I am the Source of all, ceaselessly giving;
   and I am the Soul-Force that breathes in the living.

"I am all that you love — and your loving itself;
   I am all that you need — and the meaning of wealth;
I am all that you are, and all you can be;
   and I'm all that you do, when you do it in me.

"My Kingdom is growing immeasurably fast,
   and when it is fully established, at last,
your worlds will dissolve — they're based on illusion —
   and my people redeemed from their common delusion.

"But woe to the Watchers who stand idly by
   while the slaughter goes on and the innocent die!
Woe to the shepherds and to every priest
   who would counsel my people to worship the Beast!

"For, in the end, every person will perish
   who furthers the murder of all that I cherish.
For I AM YOUR GOD," the Speaker proclaimed,

"and before me let no other lovers be named."

"Does this mean," I broke in, "that we can't avoid
  a disaster where everything must be destroyed?"

"The destruction is going on now," said the voice,
  "but as for the future — *that is your choice.*
Every prophetic warning leaves open two doors:
  one is Life, one is Death — the decision is yours.

"The door to disaster is easy and wide;
  one can hear sounds of laughter and gambling inside;
But the way into Life is a long, narrow gate:
  one has to have patience, watch closely, walk straight.

"You cannot serve two masters — it's time to decide
  - Resurrection starts now, not after you've died.
  Life can't be saved if you throw it away;
  and Satan will take those who follow his way."

Now, as the voice faded back into the night,
  I saw Christ before me, in garments of light.
His arms were stretched toward me, his hands opened wide,
  and His eyes held the whole of Creation inside.

He spoke with a voice like the sound of the sea,

with words angels heard from *eternity!*
As I listened, with heart set aflame by the Truth,
  I sensed I recovered the love of my youth!

"I, Christ, am your center, your still point of rest,
  your start and your ending, your east and your west.
I'm the Word that brings wholeness, the touch that can heal,
  the essence of fullness, the vision made real.

"I'm the newly-born infant whose first, gasping breath
  suspends it halfway between childhood and death.
I'm the innocent victim who suffers, unseen,
  yet as well I'm the substance of each living being.

"I'm your bread of community; I am the wine
  of that pruning you suffer as part of the vine.
You have only to eat of me — only to trust —
  for through me you're human; without me, you're dust.

"The Beast that you worship is everything good,
  but twisted for profit and misunderstood:

"It is courage, endurance, and genius gone sour;
  it is strength in brutality, peace won with power;
It is living for money and loving for gain;
  it is hope without sacrifice, joy without pain.

"But your courage is faith, your wisdom is love,
  your security, hoping in grace from above.
Your joy lies in justice, your worship, in caring,
  your peace, in peacemaking, your profit, in sharing...

"Your shield is the Promise that followed the Flood;
  foretold by the prophets and sealed in my Blood
when I died on the Cross so that you might be free
  to choose Life Eternal, through re-birth in Me.

"Your Mother is Grace, in her nurturing care;
  she is strength to sustain, and endurance to bear;
She is passion to carry new life in her womb,
  and compassion to stay by my side, to the tomb.

"I have sent Her to you in this time of decision --
  if you follow Her steps, you'll recover your vision.
The words that She speaks out of love and concern,
  will lead you to Me, if you're willing to learn."

I could finally hear, though it left my ears ringing,
  I could finally see, though it left my eyes stinging;
With a gaze of compassion, my Lord kept on speaking,
  refashioning, thus, the man He was seeking.

The grace of his message would finally begin
  to penetrate thresholds of barriers within,

And to shake from its temple the false deity
  of the idol of clay I had fashioned of *me*.

I witnessed inside me the crumbling to powder
  of my false inner man, while Jesus spoke, louder:
"Come to Me! Lay your burdens down here at the shore!
You'll find in the depths all you've been searching for!"

We were standing on golden sands cast from the sea,
  whose moonlit waves pounded in, incessantly,
and the surf shook the earth, splitting open the ground!
  Yet I stood there as rigid as if I were bound.

Now the gap came between us; it cracked very wide
  -- I could hear sounds of laughter and gambling inside –
And the ground at my feet turned to festering sore,
  yet I stood, bound by fear, and was sightless once more.

Finally, somehow, I tore myself free,
  preferring death, now, to this grim apathy,
And, crying, "God, save me!" I dove into space.
  - Yet as I fell, hell-bound, I felt Christ's embrace.

When I opened my eyes, we were back at the sea,
  and Christ's face was my face, and Jesus was me.

Once the vision was over, I sank down and wept,
  freed – at last – from the needs and the fears that had kept
me imprisoned for years, with the kids and my wife,
  in our neatly swept suite, seven stories from life.

And I, with eyes healed by the tears streaming down,
  saw the day's blazing light, and the highway to town.

Well, weeks had gone by since that Christmastime vision,
  when my family and I made our final decision;
Now we're inclined to a life near the street
  and we quite like the feel of the mud on our feet!

Though we're short on possessions, we use what we've got
  and, in sharing with others, we've been given a lot!
In community *(finally!)* we live, work and pray,
  and we try to serve God in a much fuller way.

When you live near the streets, it's harder, you know,
  to ignore others' needs and to let troubles go…
But the pleasure we find in our life near the earth
  is a wonderful treasure. We call it *Rebirth!*

When others ask, "How could your lives be so blessed?"
  I try to explain… But my wife says it best:

"We decided to hide in a difficult hour,
  when the fruit of our efforts turned hopelessly sour.
Had we only begun with the Kingdom in mind,
  we'd have long since received all we hunted to find.

"All we strove to achieve, all we struggled to gain,
  were as chaff in the breeze, or as dust in the rain,
'till we learned that our true strength is trust in the Lord,
  and that works based in faith bring the greatest reward."

You may wonder (I hope) what became in the end
  of our heaven-ward home. Well, I'll tell you, my friend:
Solitude's harder to find, here below!
  and though we feel deep peace wherever we go,
we chose to hang on to that "lofty abode"
  -- it's open to anyone tired of the road.

So if you're run down, and you need a retreat,
  get up off the ground to our seventh-story suite!

Four of the original eight pages of this illustrated poem are featured in the appendix of this book.

The Triumph of Innocence, Part 11:
"My Father's House" (December, 1986)

For me, a convert to Roman Catholic Christianity, 1986 was a very tough year. The Jesuit order, which I'd hoped to join in the Pacific Northwest, had gone through massive changes. Everyone I'd gotten to know was now no longer in the role they'd played before. The novitiate saw three directors within one year.

And the walk to Bethlehem, which had been initiated by members of the Jesuit Volunteer Corp, and led by their mentor Fr. Jack Morris, a Jesuit, didn't sit well with the hierarchy. Rather than count in my favor, the pilgrimage was a red flag.

Meanwhile, the Archdiocese of Seattle was, in effect, split. Donald Wuerl, a newly consecrated bishop, had been sent to relieve Archbishop Raymond G. Hunthausen of certain key duties, due to perceived irregularities. So the greatest local supporter of the Bethlehem Peace Pilgrimage, who joined us on that Good Friday when we rallied at the Trident Submarine Base, was himself being humiliated.

I decided to simplify my life. Working at a poor convalescent home, living with a community of young Catholics, and serving in local parishes, I quietly submitted my final application for the Society of Jesus. But they turned me down. Now, watching the Church seemingly caught up in politics and power-struggles, both locally and universally, yet being spiritually still of a more traditional mind-set, I projected my own internal debate onto the drama of a divided religion.

Until the 1990's, news of clerical sexual abuse of minors was very rare. Before then, countless other serious problems occupied our attention. Today's reader needs to keep in mind the tremendous damage the scandals of abuse have made to the Church's public image, its morale, and its credibility. Still, we had our share of challenges.

Feeling caught in the middle in so many ways, I invested myself in work, in spiritual growth and discernment, and in trying to stay positive. I spoke with Bishop Wuerl at one point. He explained that he also felt caught in the middle.

Unlike many of my contemporaries, I had great respect for Cardinal Ratzinger. One day, I would meet him in Menlo Park, California. Still later, I'd join brother priests in a huge gathering with him – now Pope Benedict XVI – in Rome.

Pope Benedict would appoint Donald Wuerl Archbishop of Washington D.C. in 2006, then a Cardinal in 2010. He remains in leadership today.

Raymond Hunthausen, born in 1921, is retired, and (so far as I know) in Helena, Montana, where he first served as Bishop.

From time to time, I ask my sister if she's seen him, as she lives across the street from Helena's Cathedral.

As for Pope John Paul II — well, he was a big factor in my becoming Catholic. My regard for him comes out, eventually, in this year's episode.

*This verse was understandably not well received. Most readers probably couldn't get past the first four lines. But these were designed, not to describe the deeper truths of the Catholic Church in Seattle, but rather the undeniable image projected in public. We talked about getting beyond our divisions. But the elephant in the sanctuary **was** that division. It was the inevitable confrontation between two completely distinct world-views of two increasingly polarized factions.*

And, in the end, what does it mean to be radical — to get down to the roots -- other than to witness boldly to what is most fundamentally authentic in our religion?

'Twas the night before Christmas, and all through Seattle
  the radical Catholics were still doing battle
with those for whom Truth and The Way dwell in Rome,
  whose Light is the Vatican, far, far from home.

It began when a gentle man came into town,
  and, like his Lord, turned the church upside down;
for the Spirit of Vatican 2 had possessed him
  and nothing the Romans would do could arrest him. [1]

Oh, in the beginning, he seemed orthodox,
  and he kept the lid fastened on Pandora's Box,
but 'ere long the church doors were thrown open wide
  and this bishop invited the whole world inside!

Protestants, sinners, and women poured through,
  and some say among them was Dignity, too. [2]

It seemed that more Catholics were getting divorced

---

[1] *"Vatican 2" is written this way to ensure proper pronunciation. Normally, we write "Vatican II", in Roman numerals. This Council of the Catholic Church, initiated by Pope John XXIII (serving 1958-1963), concluded in 1965. It launched a new, though in many ways unstable, era in the life of the Church. While some misinterpreted and misapplied its teachings, there were others who resisted them entirely. Now, over 50 years later, the Council's vision has yet to be fully realized.*

[2] *"Dignity" (DignityUSA) was launched in 1969 by a Californian Catholic priest and psychologist. It consisted primarily of men and women with same-sex attraction working toward greater respect and support within the Catholic Church. The movement grew quickly. In 1980, Courage International was founded for people with same-sex attraction who wished to follow the teachings of the Church regarding human sexuality, in a mutually supportive environment.*

and the bans on ex-priests were no longer enforced
the feminist movement was getting too proud
  – let alone all those things we don't mention aloud…

Then came the straw that broke all the wrong backs:
  he called Trident *"Auschwitz"* and withheld his tax!

Shock-waves went out from the Archdiocese,
  reaching Rome, bringing even the Pope to his knees,
and it seemed for the best that a small inquisition
  should be ordered to test the Archbishop's position.

Were I Joseph Ratzinger, I too would quake
  at the prospect of making a fatal mistake:

on the one hand, by letting a group of divergent
  American priests turn the whole church insurgent –
being soft where they ought to be hard to the core,
  and hard, one the issues they ought to ignore.

Writing "Pastoral Letters" that need greater scrutiny,
  and assuming "collegial" powers – that's mutiny!
(This need for democracy's such a fixation!
  We hoped it would be just a passing sensation.)

I would fear that a small lump of deviant leaven
  might keep the whole loaf from ascending to heaven;
Indeed, out of zeal I'd indulge it no longer,
  while the world goes to Hell and the Russians grow
stronger.
On the other hand, what if it went as with Boff,
  When I laid down the law, then had to back off? [3]

What would you do, when push comes to shove?
  I'd defend Mother Church in a gesture of love,
for I'd rather risk insults in service to God
  than spoil America by sparing the rod.

We've all felt the sting of that paddle, I fear,
  and the ultimate outcome has yet to appear,

---

[3]   *Leonardo Boff, a Brazilian theologian, was ordained a Franciscan priest in
1964, and completed his doctoral work in Germany in 1970. His name
became synonymous with the controversial Liberation Theology movement
which rose out of the context of repression, violence and apparent Church
complicity throughout Latin America. Due to his outspoken criticisms of
governments and of church hierarchy, together with his reference to categories
considered Marxist, he was censored by the authorities. But this seems only to
have brought greater attention to his ideas. Many other Catholic priests and
religious community leaders followed a similar trajectory in Central and South
America. Today, Boff continues as Professor Emeritus of Ethics, Philosophy
of Religion, and Ecology at the Rio de Janeiro State University.*

but when the authority's too much to bear
  I turn back to Acts, and find comfort there.

Gamaliel said, "Let the matter be dropped —
  if this movement's of God, it'll never be stopped;
if it's human, no more, it'll rot on its own,
  so for Heaven's sake, men, leave these people alone!"

The work of God's Church from the base moves along,
  and often, mere babes shame the great and the strong;
For as sure as Christ Jesus broke free of the tomb,
  this child will never crawl back in the womb!

We're impatient, I know, and we need broader vision,
  and the causes we push seem a bit like sedition,
but we've got to move forward with Vatican 2,
  and we're taught by Hunthausen in all that we do.

Never laying the blame, never seeking reward,
  he just shoulders his cross as he follows his Lord.
And though he'll insist that he's nothing sublime,
  like John Paul, his Pope, he's a saint in our time.

Oh, God! Help this Church! Only You have the cure!
  If it wasn't for Faith we would never endure.

But we know that Your Spirit will set all things right, so...

Merry Christmas to all, and to all, a good night!

Note: *the Gamaliel reference comes from Acts 5:33-39. The advice of this wise and holy Pharisee was unfortunately not followed by his best-known disciple, Saul of Tarsus. Thanks be to God, Saul would later see the Light, and become the most zealous promoter and defender of the Christian faith. For his part, Gamaliel's words are with us until the end of time. But applying them well is another question!*

Archbishop Hunthausen in the field,
Seattle Post Intelligencer, MOHAI archives

The Triumph of Innocence, Part 12:
"The Great Invitation" (December 1987)

Apparitions of the Gospa (Our Lady, that is Mary) as Queen of Peace began -- according to the six young visionaries -- on the Feast of John the Baptist (June 24) in 1981. The Bishop of Mostar began rejecting the claims early on, and due to the repressive socialist government in Yugoslavia, news of the reported sightings met with resistance. Despite all this, pilgrims to the village began pouring in.

We of the Bethlehem Peace Pilgrimage learned of Medjugorje when walking across Ireland in March of 1983. From the beginning, I felt convinced that the apparitions were authentic. I'd already learned about Mary's appearances and messages in Guadalupe (Mexico City), Lourdes (France), Fatima (Portugal) and in other locations. But here were visitations taking place now, on a daily basis.

Since I'd joined the Catholic Church just two months before the apparitions began, I felt a special connection. It seems I was riding a tidal wave of grace. It was only natural to find some way to visit the Gospa, myself.

Walking across Yugoslavia, we pilgrims would have taken a day's detour from Dubrovnik to Medjugorje, but were being strictly monitored by the authorities. And later efforts to make pilgrimage there from Ireland, in 1985, were frustrated. Now, facing an uncertain future, I spent the entire summer of 1987 in what would become, for me, a contemporary Bethlehem: a place of peace, of new hope, of re-birthing to Life.

I have changed one word in the poem. Thirty years ago, 200,000 of us gathered to celebrate the sixth anniversary of the reported apparitions. I wrote this poem in December of that same year. To help you enter the experience more fully, I've amended that reference to 2017's "thirty-six years". After all, the apparitions are still reported to be continuing daily. And the Catholic Church hierarchy has still not arrived at its final decision regarding their authenticity.

Majko Mira, moli za nas!

(ps: "Medjugorje" is pronounced "Meh-joo-**go**-ryeh", and refers to that place "between the hills". These are the Hill of Apparitions and the Hill of the Cross.)

'Twas the night before Christmas, in a land far away,
  where the people work hard with their hands every day,
where they gather to pray every evening at five,
  and to wait for the woman in gray to arrive;

'Twas the year's deepest darkness, with cold, drenching rain,
  converting to mud Medjugorje's plain;
And the people stood, soaked, as they steamed there together,
  redeeming, through praise, Yugoslavia's weather.

'Twas the eve of Christ's feast! And their hearts were on fire –
  giving glory to God was their only desire;
For their village of stone had been graced like none other
  by the love of the most-blessed one, Jesus' mother.

For thirty-six years, she had come every day,
  as she urged them to *live* peace, to fast and to pray,
calling all to conversion through six of their youth
  in simple words, pregnant with life-giving truth.

But tonight above all nights, the shared expectation
  of peasants and pilgrims from every nation,
and the anticipation of the Christ-child's returning
  made the village so radiant it seemed to be burning.

Mary came, clothed in a robe of pure light,
  with the Holy One wrapped up in dazzling white,
and though no one saw her, save those she had chosen,
  all watched in awe there, like fire held frozen.

She spoke of the future, of things soon to be,
  of a Great Invitation for Humanity,
and of Yahweh's impatience to heal his Creation --
  to restore the whole earth through a last transformation.

But she warned of a fire that all must endure –
  of purification -- Creation's sole cure –
and of torment for those who are choosing the tomb
  of attachment to that which the flames must consume.

"The table is set for a great Celebration,
  and the wedding attire is Sanctification;
I have come to invite you to feast without price
  at the side of my Child, as Bride of the Christ.

"For this," Mary cried, "Is the Hour of Grace,
  and my Son dies to gather you in his embrace!
He will come to abide with the one who believes him,
  pouring New Life into you who receive him."

Now she wept bitter tears for those who turned back,
  which streamed down her golden gown, streaking it black,
but as soon as one drop reached the Child, he stirred,
  and he turned to his mother, to utter one word.

Suddenly, all of Creation was singing;
  a billion celestial bells began ringing;
The universe pulsed like a gigantic heart,
  and its brilliant stars tore the darkness apart;

A radiant rainbow encircled the earth,
  enclosing the whole in its colorful girth,
and it wound like a gown 'round the virgin maternity
  of the one who had just given birth to Eternity.

Then once more she spoke – it was only one word;
  so softly she whispered that only he heard;
But I'd stake my life on this one wild guess:
  Her message, like Christ's – was the promise of "Yes!"

The Church of St. James, Medjugorje, and Our Lady of
Peace, Tihaljina. 2013, Rosas para la Gospa files

The Triumph of Innocence, Part 13:
"Prepare Ye the Way" (December 1988)

My wish for you, reader, is that you have at least one year in your life in which you can realize some of your more important dreams. Mine was 1988, when I reached that wonderful number, thirty-three. Winter was spent studying in beautiful Berkeley, California. On the Feast of Pentecost, I graduated from the Pacific School of Religion with a Masters in Divinity. Three days later, two friends and I had hitched a ride to Tijuana. From there we bussed to the South.

Following a month in the conflict-ridden countries of Guatemala and El Salvador, I spent another month in prayer at New Camaldoli Hermitage, near Big Sur, south of Carmel. From there, I made a retreat with Franciscans at Three Rivers, near the Sequoia forests in central California. Meanwhile, I began working with the Mir (Peace) Medjugorje Center of San Francisco. This entailed leading pilgrimages and reuniting with friends and families in what was still called Yugoslavia. We worked in a church called Guadalupe, perched on the crest of downtown San Francisco as it inclines northwestward to the Embarcadero.

Our spiritual director was a saintly, brilliant, courageous, though somewhat eccentric priest named Father Don McDonnell.

He had helped guide my hero Cesar Estrada Chavez, as the organizer launched his campaign of non-violent activism.

Fr. McDonnell was also a great enthusiast of the messages coming through Medjugorje. Over the years, his support and prayers would be instrumental in my desire to serve the people of God.

I was attracted by Franciscan spirituality, and their focus on service to the poor. Of all the Catholic religious congregations, the Franciscans also had a greater share of care for churches in the Holy Land. Beginning the process of application, I hoped — mistakenly — that my experience and work in Medjugorje would open the doors even wider. After all, the priests serving that holy site were Fransciscans.

How wrong I was. Even though I would spend the entire time of Lent at Three Rivers retreat in 1989, and take successive groups on pilgrimage to Medjugorje, before long word got out that members of the congregation from the western provinces were forbidden from going to the pilgrimage site. The Bishop of Mostar wanted the Medjugorje Franciscans replaced by diocesan clergy, and his conflicts with the order had repercussions throughout the Church.

Meanwhile, with the Iron Curtain still up, the arms race still on full bore, and warnings of the coming End Times everywhere to be heard, we were all still in apocalyptic times. Padre Pio and other mystics had shared visions of "three days of darkness" that *would herald the return of Christ. This horrendous period would amount to a kind of purge, during which the faithful were to remain sealed securely in their homes or parish churches.*

People everywhere were stocking up on emergency provisions. I didn't participate in the movement, and steered clear of the collective frenzy anticipating the end of the second millennium. But I could read the signs of the times. So the 1988 edition of the "Night before Christmas" returns to my familiar theme of a world immersed in darkness. That, after all, was the world in which we were living.

'Twas the Night before Christmas, and all through
Creation
  a trillion hearts beat in anticipation;
Billions of stars kept their watch, on and on,
  while the moon led her vigil from midnight 'till dawn.

Silence hung light in the sky like fresh snow,
  and stillness clung tight to the ground down below;
Not a creature dared stir on the face of the earth,
  for the whole world was pregnant, and soon to give birth.

The Signs of the Times had, at last, become clear,
  and those who weren't waiting were quaking in fear;
For the Innocent One who was born in that hour
  would now be returning in Glory and Power.

As for me? I was home, on my knees, on the floor,
  searching for pennies I'd stashed long before --
Not much of a spender, I'd tried to protect
  those funds that my Lender might come to collect.

Suddenly all of my hair stood up straight;
  my heart pounded, loud, at a frightening rate;
A brilliant flash split the night far and wide,
  and a thunderous crash shook the whole countryside.

A chorus of song rose in cheerful ascent
  while a vast, screaming throng made its fearful descent;
The sun was extinguished; the moon turned blood red,
  and the heavens rolled up like a scroll, overhead,

But just then my pennies rolled back into view;
  exclaiming, "Thank Goodness!" I snatched up a few.
Escaping the Chaos, I dove into bed,
  pulled over the covers, and buried my head.

For three darkened days, we lay hidden like sheep,
  my pennies and I, in our refuge of sleep --
And God only knows what the scene was outside
  -- I knew enough just to shut up and hide!

On the fourth morning, a new silence fell,
  and I sensed myself torn between Heaven and Hell;
A freezing sweat drenched me, like dense, winter mist,
  while the coins turned to ice in my tightly clenched fist.

"Christ! Come and save me!!" I heard myself scream,
  and the words bounced around me, as if in a dream;
But as soon as that echoing sounded no more,
  a firm, gentle knocking began at the door.

"Who are you?" I choked. He said, "It is I".
  -- With my heart in my throat, I was ready to die!
"The door, Lord, is bolted -- but come in," I said;
  "I Am," He replied, from the side of my bed.

Now, somehow, my whole being warmed from within,
  while the coins turned so hot, they were burning my skin!
So ignoring their value, I dropped them right there:
  "Lord, here are the talents you left to my care."

And now, in sheer terror, unable to budge,
  I rolled my eyes backwards to gaze at my Judge;
But when all the covers had slipped off my head,
  I saw, not His Wrath, but Compassion instead.

With pain in His features, and blood on His side,
  He said, "Child of God, it was for you I died."

"I chose you for Life from the very Beginning,
  and I kept you from death when you wouldn't stop sinning.
I gave you great freedom, the graces to lead you;
  My Blood to redeem and My Body to feed you.

"My Mother had nurtured you clear from the start,
  and she shed many tears to develop your heart;

Your future was safe in our Hands 'till the day
  you decided, in pride, to create it *your* way.

"We offered our Love when you didn't have any;
  you traded it off in exchange for a penny.
What you had at conception you've already lost,
  and you've saved a few cents at a terrible cost.

"I would prune you away as a branch that has withered,
  but my Mother has prayed that your soul be delivered.
She's asked me to send you, as servant and friend,
  to tell all the earth that I'm coming again."

..."But, Lord!" I protested, "You're already here!"
  "That's right," He replied. "And My Triumph is near."
"But Lord, I'm unworthy -- the world's poorest priest!"
  "My Mother," He said, "always chooses the least."

"I understand nothing," I had to confess.
  He asked, **"Do you love me?"** I cried out, **"Yes!"**

Just then, a blinding white light filled the room!
  There was nothing that love-fire didn't consume!

I felt my whole life being turned right around
  as my house made of withered works burned to the ground.[1]

Next, I was shouting, "Make way for the Lord!!"
  and I found myself wielding a double-edged sword.
I scattered the ash of my past with one blow,
  then, looking for demons, ran out in the snow.

Had it not been for brothers, who slept near the site,
  I'd have fought for my Mother the rest of the night;
As it was, they awoke me by slapping my face,
  then they poured Holy Water all over the place.

My feet were half frozen from lack of protection,
  yet, worse still, my head seemed in need of correction.
So they gave me a long psychological test,
  recommending, thereafter, a very long rest.

Well... I've never yet heeded advice of this kind,
  so long as that dream remains fresh in my mind;
What talents I have, I'm investing in full
  for the good of the world and the sake of my soul.

---

[1]   *See 1 Corinthians 3:11-21. This scripture foretells a divine fire which will test all works done on the foundation of faith in Jesus Christ. For those whose works are consumed by the fire, there is still the hope of salvation, because the foundation remains. Catholics understand this passage to support the concept of Purgatory.*

I know Christ is coming -- *the Hour is late!*
  May He take His Creation, and set it all straight!
I might seem fanatic, but, man, I'm not slack,
  for I plan to be ready when Jesus comes back.

So if someone should ever add stress to your day
  by crying, *"Repent!"* and *"Prepare ye the Way!"*
Don't pass up the offer as far too extreme:
  you may have to suffer a similar dream!

Image of Divine Mercy by Fratelli Bonella, wjhirten.com

The Triumph of Innocence, Part 14:
"The Key" (December 1989)

Father Jozo (Joseph) Zovko, a charismatic Franciscan who had paid a high price for supporting Medjugorje's visionaries from the start, invited me to work with him in June of 1989. Anka, his interpreter and a friend of mine, had introduced us when I brought a group of Pilgrims to his parish in Tihaljina ("Tee-hah-**lee**-nah").

Returning with another group in August, I sent them on their way States-ward and remained in Medjugorje. This initiated six months of association and service with "Fra" Jozo. I never learned Serbo-Croatian, but we managed to communicate in Italian and my few words of German. Anka, too, was on hand to translate.

Together with three other assistants from Europe, Anka and I would greet the pilgrims, attend to their needs, and lead worship in preparation for Father Jozo's inspiring talks. The gathering of pilgrims from around the world continued daily from Monday through Saturday, from 7:00am until late in the afternoon. Even on Sundays, pilgrims showed up, often unannounced. Fr. Jozo never refused to meet with them and to share a reflection or prayers.

In the course of my stay, hundreds of thousands of visitors had come, and left deeply inspired. This was, for me, a confirmation that, despite all my negative experiences and frustrations with institutions and individuals within the Church, Jesus was still very present among His people. And His Mother, Mary, was there, gathering her children. Among them, I was present, and wrote this year's poem in that parish.

This year's story doesn't refer directly to world events. But just over the horizon, the world was changing rapidly. One by one, nations once chained to the Soviet Union were breaking free. With Father Jozo, I sat evenings to watch the latest on yet another country which had overturned its socialist regime. One day, after coverage of the bloodiest revolution, that of Rumania (in which over 1,000 died), Fra Jozo turned to me and said: **"It will not be so easy for us."**

This poem doesn't mention the geo-political situation. There wasn't much I could do about that, anyway. Still searching for my place in the Church, I needed to focus once again on the problem of an incomplete conversion. Perhaps, if I could get this one job finished, I might have more to offer a broken world.

'Twas the night before Christmas, in wee Tihaljina,
  at the height of a very deep Christmas novena,
and we huddled together, like sheep in a stall,
  -- so silent, so still, you could hear the snow fall.

Such a diligent vigil I never have kept
  in that small, chilly chapel where, often, I slept
at the foot of our Lord, when I ought to have prayed
  -- but *this* night, excitement could come to my aid.

The bleak 1980's would soon yield their place
  to a decade unequalled in Life-giving Grace
since the days of our Savior's miraculous birth,
  and His Passion that transformed the face of the earth.

Singing, we lingered in long adoration
  as we knelt, face-to-Face, with the Lord of Creation;
Our souls shared humanity's infinite thirst,
  while our hearts felt so joyful, it seemed they would burst!

The hour grew late, and the snow, very deep,
  and I sensed, in my depths, I was falling asleep;
So I pondered the graces I'd like to receive
  and the glorious things I would hope to achieve.

Then, lo! The Christ-child was here, in our midst!
 – with a tiny gold key in His miniature fist.
He shone like the sun in His Mother's embrace,
 and the room was illumined by light from His Face.

So brilliant was He that our hearts were on fire!
 So beautiful, She, that we glowed with desire!
And like the disciples on Tabor's great height,
 we fell, overwhelmed by this wonderful sight.

Then Mary spoke, just as our vision went dim:
 "This is my beloved Son: follow Him!"
I cried out for help, at the very last minute;
 she took my hand, and put something in it.

When at last I awoke to the dawn's early rays,
 and angelic hosts singing Glory and Praise,
I opened two half-swollen eyes to behold
 my friends still at prayer 'round a monstrance of gold.

And there, in the center, as plain as could be,
 the Bread of Life patiently waited for me.

"You've slept through our vigil, again," whispered one,
 as she pointed outside to the light of the sun;

"But we've pleaded with Jesus, Who's here in this Host,
   to enlighten your mind with the grace you need most."

Ashamed, I remained with my face to the floor,
   unable to move for an hour or more.
I'd been bathing in glory, before, when I slept –
   but now I felt hopelessly poor, and I wept.

My eyes filled with tears when I saw how my dreams
   had been driving me years in pursuit of extremes:
Climbing up mountain peaks, flying to the sun,
   I'd run from the valley of the Suffering One.

My life had been spent in a quest for a prize
   that would rise up, then vanish in front of my eyes;
And the higher I leapt, the harder the ground --
   for even the Transfigured Christ came back down!

I realized the ultimate summit would be
   not Everest's crest, but instead: Calvary.
With this recognition, a sense of release
   and a flood of God's Love filled my whole soul with peace.

I rose to my knees to continue in prayer
   with the friends who, like cedars, were still rooted there;

And, lo! In my fist was a tiny gold key!
and on it was written: *"Luke 9:23"*. [1]

O Lord! Take our lives! And make them Your own;
give new hearts of flesh for the old ones of stone!
Be born in us, Christ-child, our fresh Inspiration,
and come in Your Glory -- Redeem your Creation!!

And You, Blessed Mother, conceived without sin,
through Whom Christ first came, and is coming again;
Come, take our hands! Illumine our way!
and guide us to Life 'till that very last Day! Amen.

---

[1] *See Luke 9:23-27. This passage immediately precedes the Transfiguration of*
Christ (9:28-36). It is given by way of indicating a disciple's path: knowing
that Jesus is the Lord of Glory, in this world we still follow Him as the
Crucified One. I received this citation (Luke 9:23) spontaneously when
composing this line of the poem, without knowing what it contained. Since
then, my principal challenge has been in living it out. So it goes, I suppose,
for all of us who call ourselves "Christian".

The Triumph of Innocence, Part 15:
"The Star" *(December 1990)*

Soon, Slovenia and Croatia would be declaring independence from Yugoslavia. Fra Jozo's predictions of a bloody, drawn-out war would come true. The seceding republics would choose June 25, 1991: the tenth anniversary of that first day when the Gospa spoke, calling for peace -- and promising peace to those who would heed her messages. The first rumblings of conflict were palpable while I still lived in Bosnia Herzegovina. But before long, I would exchange Tihaljina for Tijuana.

In formation with Mother Teresa's Missionary of Charity Fathers in Mexico, I had found my vocational home. From the Pacific Northwest, and then so many places to the East, I had finally moved South. My feet were finally planted in one place.

This, the last of my Christmas stories, grew naturally out of our experience working with the poor just south of the border. Those who struggled day by day simply to survive didn't have time or energy to absorb themselves in the deplorable state of the world. Looking northward, they hoped somehow to provide for their children and to escape the cycles of poverty, corruption and violence.

In my work at Tijuana's General Hospital, I watched family after family deal with the harsh realities of homelessness, illness, abandonment, and despair. And that dilemma would only get worse over time. Within a few years, the Casa de Migrantes, once full of the homeless and people hoping to cross the northern border, would fill up instead with people who had been deported. And today, twenty-seven years since I moved to Mexico, things look more bleak than ever.

May God be present in this time of refugees and immigrants seeking sanctuary, especially for those who've already suffered beyond description. May we shine for them with the Light of Christ! And may they somehow find the welcome they need — this side of Heaven's gates.

'Twas the Night before Christmas, not far to the South,
  where the land opens wide like a gigantic mouth
to swallow the poor, as they follow the light
  that shines on the northern horizon -- so bright!

For decades, they've journeyed from lands near and far,
  drawn on by the sight of that beautiful star
whose radiant face turns the night into day,
  just north of the border -- yet so far away.

The poor stood there, motionless, lined at the gate,
  yearning to enter, but having to wait,
while the solemn gate-keepers, with legal precision,
  examined each case, and made their decision.

Yet the glittering beacon continued to call,
  speaking "Freedom!", "Prosperity!", "Justice for all!"
And beneath that gold orb, with its glow so entrancing,
  one could hear sounds of caroling, laughter, and
  dancing.

Oh, here was a dreamland of milk and of honey,
  where one could find comfort, the good life, and
  money!
But between Poor and Promised Land stood a Great
Wall,
  and most were locked out, with no promise at all.
- - - - - - - - - -
I know a young couple who, forced to turn back,
  are living alone in a small plywood shack.
Having fled from El Salvador's merciless war,
  they'd escaped with their clothes and their wounds --
nothing more.

Now they had nothing but faith in their Lord,
  hope for the future, and Love as the cord

that would bind them together in Christ, come what may
--
    They were wed to the Cross from the very first day.

Maria had just given birth to a boy,
    and the sight of this Christmas gift filled them with
    joy;
They named him Emmanuel, in their delight --
    but the poor child died on that very same night.

What cruel irony! That so close to the border
    an infant should die of a simple disorder,
and that this should happen on the Christ-child's feast!
    Hearts broken, they gazed at their baby, deceased.

 And so, once again, they were washed by those tears
    which had been their inheritance, so many years;
And they cried out in anguish to Christ and His Mother,
    and, begging for mercy, they held one another.

It seemed all Creation was gathered as one,
    to unite in this plea for their innocent son;
And the world seemed to stop -- it could not carry on --
    too many lost children extinguish the dawn!

By midnight, the silence had settled so deep

that their weeping gave way to a moment of sleep;
Yet this minute brought grace that will bear fruit forever,
    for within it two broken hearts grew back together.

For their night-blackened shack became brilliant white
    as a woman appeared in a cascade of light;
She was mantled in turquoise, and stood on the moon,
    and her radiant face changed the midnight to noon.

She remained but an instant, but while she was there,
    she picked up the child with infinite care,
and said, ***"In the Name of My Son, Come to Life!"***
    And she handed him back to José and his wife.

When the couple awoke, they gazed at the bed
    where, hours before, they had left him for dead,
and they found little Manuel, eyes opened wide,
    with marks on his hands and his feet, and his side.

The look in his eyes was as deep as the sea,
    and, in his expression, profound ecstasy;
The room was illumined by light from his face,
    and the fragrance of roses anointed the place.

Transported by what they had witnessed and heard,
    the two didn't see that the boy never stirred;

For the perfume they breathed was his spirit, set free
  -- Our Lady had called him to Eternity.

For hours, the family remained stationed there,
  the child, in heaven, his parents, in prayer,
while the dawn of Christ's feast day began to unfold
  in crimson, and turquoise, and brilliant gold.

Yet already, thousands were gathered outside --
  They had come from the North, with a light as their
  guide;
For above them had risen a glorious Star
  which outshines the northerly beacon by far.

Looks are deceiving, says Wisdom of old;
  all that glitters may not be celestial gold;
And for all of its luster, the North-Star was made
  by humanity's hands: one day it must fade.

But the Morning Star, lifting Her radiant Face
  is ascending, with Christ, through the Power of Grace.
In the Dawn's early stirring, God's Life-giving Breath
  is creating New Life from the ashes of death.

And the Star of the Poor is a Southerly one,
  and it shines, East to West, with the Light of the Son.

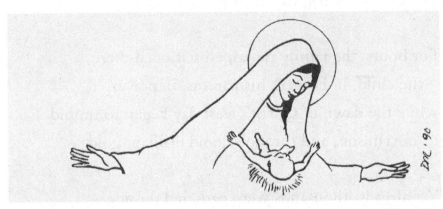

THE PEOPLE WHO WALK IN DARKNESS HAVE SEEN A GREAT LIGHT

FOR UNTO US A CHILD IS BORN, A SON IS GIVEN (Is.9:5)

From a Christmas Card made by the author in 1990 as a part of the Missionary of Charity Fathers, co-founded by Mother Teresa. It was created at the same time as the last episode of 1990. Upper picture of Mary adapted from a design for Medjugorje (MIR) Center of San Francisco by Kim Yap, around 1988.

After-Words of the Author

Dear Reader, **Congratulations! You've survived** – at least *this* journey.

The fifteen-year segment chronicled by these Christmas stories described, in a sketchy way, one-third of my life. Beginning with my first year at the Academy of the Rockies in Idaho (1973-4), and culminating in my years with the Missionaries of Charity (1990-93), these were twenty years of searching, of the vision-quest, of trading in the innocence of early life for the experience of a world traveler.

But, as the poems increasingly indicated, the experience I sought was not that of horizontal, but rather *vertical* movement. That explains why you found so much reference to going up-and-down – even to the point of having to fetch King Kong from atop the majestic Statue of Liberty.

In our spiritual lives, we're usually focused on the ascent. We don't just climb the mountain of faith *"because it's there"*. We climb to overcome our fallen human nature, which drags us down. We're hardwired to see heaven as *"up there"* where the air is purer and more rarified. We feel lighter on the heights, as if gravity has less dominion, the higher we rise.

Scripture and the history of spirituality all seem to confirm this fundamental movement of religion. But they also testify to something even greater.

As we progress in the things of God, we learn that the old adage is also true for us: *"Whatever goes up, must come down"*.

This means that one's ascent of the mountain does not end at the peak.

In the Christian life – as with all authentic spirituality – one has to descend again to the valley.

One has to bring down the stone tablets of God's revelation for humanity *(Exodus 32:15)*.

One must leave the luminescent mists of the Transfiguration to serve again at the base, and even to stand beside the Lamb who must be condemned and crucified *(Luke 9:37, 22:39)*.

One must "Go out to all the world" with the Good News, rather than vigil on the hilltop for Jesus to come back, someday, to clean up our mess *(Matthew 28:19, Mark 16:15, Acts 1:11)*.

One must, having discovered ancient treasures, bring them home again to share with others who haven't had the opportunity, ability, or vision to hunt them down. [1]

This is what God did for us in the Incarnation. It is called *"Kenosis"*.

Translated by Saint Paul, it means: *"Have this mind among yourselves, which is yours in Christ Jesus, who, though he was in the form of God, did not count equality with God a thing to be grasped, but emptied himself, taking the form of a servant, being born in the likeness of men.*

And being found in human form he humbled himself and became obedient unto death, even death on a cross.

Therefore God has highly exalted him and bestowed on him the name which is above every name, that at the name of Jesus every knee should bow, in heaven and on earth and under the earth, and every tongue confess that Jesus Christ is Lord, to the glory of God the Father." [2]

So be it. Asi Sea. Fiat Voluntas Tua. Amen!

Maranatha, Come, Lord Jesus!

---

[1] *See Matthew 13:44, Acts 4:35, and the Hero legends of so many cultures.*

[2] *Philippians 2:5-11 (RSV)*

Credits for photographs used in this book

Every effort has been made to give credit for photographs and to obtain permission for their use. Any oversights in this area are unintentional.

Page 89: AP FILE - This Sept. 10, 1987 file photo shows President Ronald Reagan and Pope John Paul II talking as they walk during a visit by the pope to the United States. Polish officials have unveiled a statue of former President Ronald Reagan and John Paul II, honoring two men whom many Poles credit with helping to topple communism in Gdansk on Saturday July 14, 2012. The bronze statue, is a slightly larger than life rendering of the two late leaders. It is based on this Associated Press photograph taken in 1987 on John Paul's second pontifical visit to the U.S. (AP Photo/Scott Stewart, File)

Page 125: Photograph of a magnet created by, and available through, Santa Cruz, CA based "Peacemonger". Permission granted for use in this book. Visit http://www.peacemonger.org/assets/images/products/ FM041_-_Eisenhower_Quote.jpg or call (855) 657-3223

P. 151: Archbishop Hunthausen's photograph was published in the Seattle Post Intelligencer in 2015, and is archived through Seattle's Museum of History and Industry. Permission granted by MOHAI. The links: http://blog.seattlepi.com/seattlepolitics/files/2015/04/hunthausen.jpg

https://mohai.org/collections-and-research/#order-photos.

P. 156: https://rosasparalagospa.files.wordpress.com/2013/10/gospa-parroquia.jpg

P. 165: This version of the Divine Mercy Image is sold by W. J. Hirten Wholesale Religious Products, under Item Number (810-123).

Appendix:
Four original pages from episode of 1985

I include the following excerpts from "The Seventh Story Suite" to give you some idea of how the stories looked when they first came out. This episode, as you can tell, took eight pages of single-spaced typing, along with the illustrations. I hope you get some sense for how it felt to read these sagas for the first time, as they were responding to current events in the world and in my life, and to issues of ultimate concern for people in every country.

Regarding the Meter of these poems

My choice, from the beginning, to follow the metric pattern of "A Visit from Saint Nicholas" was not accidental. This structure of language is exceptionally well-suited for epic stories. Far from the lockstep of iambic pentameter (da-Dah, da-Dah, da-Dah, da-Dah, da-Dah), the format Moore chose was far more versatile and attractive. It's no coincidence that my favorite children's author, Dr. Suess, often used this structure as well.

According to our beloved Wikipedia, "Anapestic tetrameter is a poetic meter that has four anapestic metrical feet per line. Each foot has two unstressed syllables followed by a stressed syllable. It is sometimes referred to as a 'reverse dactyl', and shares the rapid, driving pace of the dactyl".

This meter carries you along like a galloping horse, like the theme song to The Lone Ranger (from Rossini's William Tell Overture).

If that doesn't help, imagine yourself engaged in a never-ending waltz across a moonlit meadow with a light summer breeze. The 1-2-3, 1-2-3, 1-2-3, 1-2-3, almost sing-song rhythm allows you to stay with the dance forever. All you have to do is take your first step on the "3", and you're off on the journey. Who is your partner? That's yours to answer.

The Triumph of Innocence, part 9

This year, a once-ordinary, now-alienated couple have difficulty getting back "down to earth". They had suffered somewhat in the course of life, and didn't want any more of that! So they have been hiding behind "religion" and the security of an insulated world. But, thanks be to God, help arrives in extraordinary ways.

This also represents a personal effort to "come down" off some unusual forms of peace-work and to re-integrate into the more common aspects of life.

I would gladly have written more about the Soviet Union, etc., but...these verses seem to force themselve on me--I only struggle with rhymes and meter.

To help with your reading and rythme, I've spaced phrases from one another, at times, or, rarely, added a dot (•) before words upon which you should land with force. As in: 'Twas the •night before...

Please read page one with a tone of condescension (like a flawless and lofty preacher), and, if you remember, the last page-and-a-half like a country bumpkin.

Thanks to all of you who supported, in any way, the last few year's worth of peace-walking and connected activities. I feel tremendous gratitude for all the experiences and meetings which have been possible through your assistance.

THE SEVENTH-STORY SUITE

'Twas the·night before Christmas, and all through our town
Not a creature was still! --they were running around
Like a loosed coop of chickens being chased late at night
--And I gazed from my roost with considerable fright.

The crunch of fast footsteps on fresh-fallen snow,
The sound of loud pounding on doors down below,
And the shouting and honking that echoed around,
Left the Spirit of Christmas nowhere to be found.

But I, not one lightly to jeopardize life,
Climbed right back to bed and the arms of my wife.

We were•seven stories up from the earth's broken sod,
So much •closer to Heaven, the wholeness of God.
We abode with our children in peaceful repose,
Unaffected--we hoped--by the world and its woes.

Always kind to our friends, giving alms to the poor,
We led quiet lives of prayer, and we asked nothing more.

Oh, of course, long ago, we had felt greater zeal
For existence below, in the world they call "real",
But the specter of death and the trials of life
Had shred our ideals like a double-edged knife;
And so we'd retired to our high seventh-story,
Where we waited for Christ to return in his Glory.

Taking refuge, therefore, in our lofty estate,
We now prayed for the chaos below to abate.

I had seen a great crowd from all nations, bowed down
To a hideous beast with a five-sided crown.

All around it lay bones it had spat in the field,
And over it arched an invulnerable shield.
Its left hand clutched money; its right held a sword,
And it thundered, "I AM!!", while the crowd echoed, "-LORD!"

Then came this vision: a billion faces
Made up of all ages, all nations, all races;
They were thin with starvation and pale with disease;

Said a whispering voice from behind: "I am these".

And then the voice cried, 'ere this vision was done:
"Why do you hide from my people--my son??"

Needless to say, I was deeply distressed,
And those echoing words left me weak and depressed,
So that, speechless, I lay cold as ice in the snow
'Till my wife, who was also blind, cried, "Dear--let's go!"

We groped through the darkness and rose to our feet,
Only hoping by chance to find friends in the street;
And friends we did find!--our three children, in fact--
Somehow the great flash had left their sight intact.

They led us along at a shuffling pace
Toward a hill where the light had now taken its place.

When we finally arrived, there were sounds of a crowd
(that is, whispering, sighing, and praying aloud)
And the voice of a woman who called us by name,
Saying, "I am called Anna. Thank God that you came.

"Tonight I was given a frightening vision
And a warning that this is the Day of Decision.
I told all your neighbors that Christ would appear,
But you were too high and too hidden to hear."

"In the days of the Great Flood, when Evil was purged
From the face of Creation, my son Noah urged
Me to wipe away even the option for sin,
So a new and more promising world might begin.

How deeply I yearned to free Earth from this bind!
-To take back the choice which I gave humankind!
But to do that would only have made matters worse
by throwing the process of Life in reverse.

Evolution and growth is the work of Creation,
And Life to the full is its sole Destination.
To enslave human freedom would cripple the soul
--But when you return to me, I want you whole.

I've made you unable to live to the full
Unless you cleave to me with body and soul;
The Paradox, then, is that I make you free,
Yet your·true freedom lies in allegiance to me.

I gave you my pledge in the covenant arc
That life would continue, no matter how dark
And how petty your motives and actions might be
--So if ·Holocaust threatens, do not blame me!

My Kingdom is growing immeasurably fast,
And when it is fully established, at last,
Your worlds will dissolve--they're based on illusion--
And my people redeemed from their common delusion.

But woe to the Watchers who stand idly by
While the slaughter goes on and the innocent die!
Woe to the Warlords and to every priest
Who would counsel my people to worship the Beast!

For, in the end, every human will perish
Who furthered the murder of all that I cherish."

"-Does this mean," I broke in, "That we can't avoid
A disaster where everything must be destroyed?"

"The disaster is going on now," said the voice,
"But as for the future--that is your choice.

"Every prophetic warning leaves open two doors:
One is Death, one is Life--the decision is yours.

The door to disaster is easy and wide;
One can hear sounds of laughter and gambling inside;
But the Way into Life is a long, darkened gate:
One has to have patience, watch closely, walk straight.

5

```
You may wonder (I hope) what became in the end
Of our heavenly home--well, I'll tell you, my friend:
Solitude's harder to find, here below!
-And though we feel deep peace wherever we go,
We chose to hang onto  that "lofty abode"
--It's open to anyone  tired of the road.

So if you're run down  and you need a retreat,
Get up off the ground  to our seventh-story suite!!
```

Amen

8

Ah, you have the patience of Job to have endured this verse.

Please share it around. And if you have any questions, suggestions, complements or complaints, write me c/o 4204 NE 50, Seattle, Wa. 98105.

May this coming year bring us all deeper into the work of God's Kingdom, and much closer to the fullness of Christ.   Thanks.   —Dean McRath—

The final page of author's 1985 original Triumph of Innocence,
"The Seventh Story Suite"

187

CPSIA information can be obtained
at www.ICGtesting.com
Printed in the USA
BVOW09*2041100717

488819BV00005B/21/P